Stranded On Earth

The Story of a
Roswell Crash Survivor

by Commander Sanni Emyetti Ceto

Earth Star Publications

Stranded On Earth
The Story of a Roswell Crash Survivor

Commander Sanni Emyetti Ceto

Earth Star Publications
Pagosa Springs, Colorado

FIRST EDITION printing June 2004
Second Printing July 2004
Third Printing September 2004
Fourth Printing April 2005
Fifth Printing November 2006
Sixth Printing September 2008
Seventh Printing October 2009

ISBN 0-944851-22-3

Printed in the United States of America

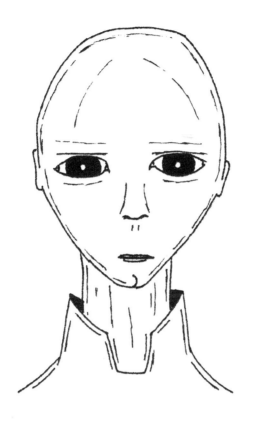

Commander Ceto in Zeti form

Contents

Foreword *by Dr. R. Leo Sprinkle* 5

Chapter 1. **One Stormy Night** 9

Chapter 2. **Stranded** 17

Chapter 3. **The Social Workers** 25

Chapter 4. **On My Own** 37

Chapter 5. **The Difficult Years** 45

Chapter 6. **Rocky Mountain High** 53

Chapter 7. **A New Life** 61

Chapter 8. **Leaving the Old Behind** . .67

Chapter 9. **Return to Roswell** 75

Chapter 10. **Bingo** 87

Chapter 11. **Events** 91

Chapter 12. **The Home World** 113

Afterword 123

The Author 127

Foreword

Welcome to the world of Marcellina Beckwith, a woman who is both human and extraterrestrial (E.T.). Welcome to the world of Commander S.E. Ceto, a Zeti scientist whose craft crashed on Earth. Welcome to the world of Sanni Ceto, who serves as a link between these two lifetimes, and who provides a bittersweet story about being "stranded on Earth."

If you, as reader, are puzzled by this introduction, then relax: The story unfolds nicely. If your mind boggles as you read this book, be aware of any tendency to jump to a convenient conclusion.

If you talk to others about this book, be aware of their reactions: Are they accepting or rejecting of your comments? Are they interested? Ambivalent? Angry? Curious? Sarcastic? Thoughtful? Willing to learn more?

Be aware that when I first learned about Sanni, I asked myself a variety of questions. Then, I asked Sanni many questions, in telephone and radio interviews with Mr. Roy Timm, and others. Sanni has replied with information that is both simple and elegant: Simple in human understanding, and elegant in cosmic explanation.

When you are ready, ask yourself a question: What if *(gasp!)* Sanni *is* who she says she is? What if she *is* a hybrid human/E.T., who remembers a previous lifetime as a crew commander whose ship crashed on Earth, whose leaders arranged this lifetime, partly as a penance for a lapse in judgment, but also as an opportunity to share her knowledge with those around her?

I am grateful for the opportunity to learn from Sanni. I am pleased with the efforts of Sanni, her friends, and her editor, Ann Ulrich Miller, to bring this information to us.

I look forward to the opportunity to meet Sanni in person, and to speak further with her about her life and her work: Sharing Love and Light.

— *R. Leo Sprinkle, Ph.D., Counseling Psychologist,*
Professor Emeritus,
Counseling Services, University of Wyoming
Author of *Soul Samples: Personal Explorations in*
Reincarnation and UFO Experiences,
Columbus, N.C.: Granite Publishing

Special Thanks

I would like to thank all of my friends for their help in bringing me a new life, and for their friendship in helping me become the light worker I am guided to be.

Special thanks to Starhawk and to my friend Jack, who moved me and my cats to Colorado. I would especially like to thank Ann Ulrich for her support in standing by me and encouraging me in this difficult process of producing this book.

For those of you on the Internet who know how I write — spelling phonetically rather than in correct English — I thank you for your patience and your support. The words in this book have been edited to make for easier reading.

I would also like to thank Carol Syska for her friendship in helping me reconnect with my past at Roswell, and Dr. Leo Sprinkle for his encouragement and support, as well as UFO researcher Mr. Roy Timm, for all the love and support and his eagerness to learn about other societies beyond Earth.

I wish to honor the following crew members who lost their lives in the crash at Roswell: Lorkiah, Naylaiu, Shienyah and Kaiyha, and the twelve scientists who went down in nearby Socorro. The pain of their loss has weighed heavily upon me, and I honor each and every one of them.

Commander Sanni Emyetti Ceto

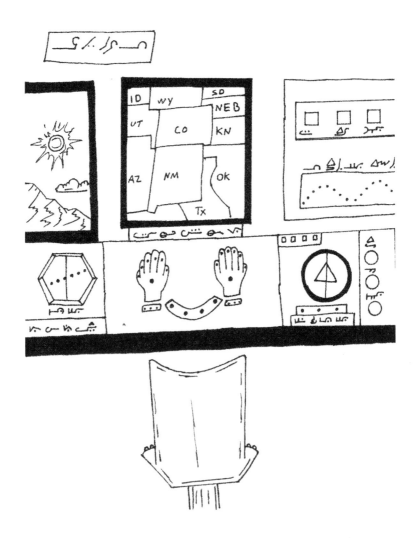

An inside view of my ship's controls

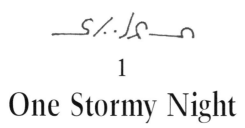

1
One Stormy Night

The night cycle was upon us. We cruised dangerously near the military base. In the distance there was a turbulent thunderstorm battering the atmosphere. Brilliant flashes of electricity erupted spontaneously — here, there and all around — unpredictable and shattering.

"The mother ship is signaling," announced Naylaiu (Nay-loo). "They are asking that we retreat."

Without emotion I stared at my screen. It was my duty to maintain defenses. My mind interfaced with the computer at all times during flight. To break that concentration — even for a moment — could spell disaster.

"Tell them we acknowledge," I told Naylaiu.

My ship was on a purely scientific mission to study, observe and collect living specimens. In our storage compartments we had live animals, plants, rocks, soil and water to take back with us to the Home World. We had collected mostly single-celled animals, bacteria, mold and such, and had advanced up to birds, small mammals and fish. On the Home World we would bioengineer these specimens to adapt them to our planet and our environment.

Naylaiu projected her thoughts again to me. She was deeply concerned. "Lieutenant, these facilities have all been catalogued. I suggest we leave the area. That storm over the desert is extremely ominous."

It was, in fact, the worst storm we had encountered on

the Terran world. We didn't know at the time that humans were experimenting with a new kind of radar technology. I stood at my computer console with my arms outstretched and my hands up against the tilted screen. I did not look at Naylaiu, but tried to reassure her. "We won't be in any danger, Naylaiu. I just want to have a closer look."

"They won't pick us up on their radar," Kiayha (Ki-ya) reminded us, "but there is always danger of observation when our ships come this close."

The other two crew members, Shienyah (Shen-ya) and Lorkiah (Lor-ka), stood behind me as they concentrated on their panels. They said nothing, but I detected their concern as well. Still, I wanted to fly over the base.

The crew of five aboard my ship that crashed

The lightning storm was now in full force. The sky danced with electrical surges and angry clouds billowed and threatened the cowering earth below. To me it was an exciting spectacle and we were in the midst of it. I guided our little delta-shaped craft even nearer to that which was forbidden.

"Sanni, the shadow ship is signaling again," Naylaiu informed me. "They want us to pull away... now."

The protective forcefield that surrounded our ship, as well as the sister craft that was following us, was in my total control. It was our life line to safety and security in this major electrical event. I suppose a part of me — the thrill seeker — was what had led me to dare coming this close.

We were not supposed to be there. As a matter of fact, we were violating the orders of the Council by coming to Earth in the first place. Earth was strictly off-limits to all space craft, but my desire to lead a specimen-collecting scientific expedition there had been just too tempting to let a little thing such as Federation rules and regulations stop me.

My crew of four colleagues had tried to talk me out of this, but in the end I had convinced them it was safe and we would get away with it. After all, it wasn't my first field trip. We had been on five flights beforehand. And the ship behind us, sharing the forcefield, had agreed to accompany us against their commander's better judgment, because they knew I had succeeded at ignoring the establishment before.

Being scientists from Zeta Reticuli, we were all indelibly curious by nature. A series of nuclear tests being performed around White Sands and in the ocean on Earth had attracted the attention of many in space. Humans on Earth were playing around with Atom. They were detonating bombs and they did not realize the consequences of their actions.

These detonations were what had originally led our people to Earth, to observe and to study. We wanted to know why Earth people were performing nuclear tests and why they would use this technology for war purposes instead of peaceful endeavors.

As a result, we came and studied all of Earth's cultures, all the different languages, and visited all the major cities. We made several flyovers of this particular desert region before the Council made the decision to quarantine the planet.

"Sanni, I think we should break away." There was urgency in Naylaiu's telephathic words. "Please..."

Shienyah behind me shrieked. "Look at that!" she cried.

"What is it?" asked Lorkiah.

Startled by their interaction, I turned my head to see what Shienyah was indicating on her panel, and just at that moment the connection to my computer was interrupted. The forcefield went down.

In that split second a bolt of lightning hit us. When the forcefield went down, the field surrounding the entire vehicle was left vulnerable. This caused electricity in the atmosphere to be drawn to the hull of the ship. The sister craft behind us went down first. A second later, the discharge of electricity was attracted to our hull, just like a moth to a flame, and then we went down.

All I remember is a loud explosion and a brilliant white light that filled our entire craft.

The next thing I remember is lying on my back on the cold, damp ground. I was facing up toward the dark sky and behind me was a huge boulder. I could see the stars between some drifting clouds, and cold raindrops pelted my body. All around me were the pitiful cries from my four crew members. They were in pain and they continued to wail and cry for what seemed an eternity.

Then everything grew silent. The smoke smell was thick

in the night air, and I detected ozone from the burning instruments that had been aboard my ship. The quiet was unnerving. I tried to move, but I could barely lift my finger or turn my head. I couldn't move my leg or arm on my left side, and it hurt really bad. I knew that my head was injured from the horrible pain. I faded in and out of consciousness.

The rain came and went. Eventually it stopped altogether. I remember losing consciousness briefly, but feeling as though something brought me out of it. It was a sort of warmth, and it caused me to open my eyes. I saw a star in the sky, coming up over the horizon, and I remember thinking how odd that there was only one star — not two — and then recalled that this was Earth and not my home world. On my world there are two day stars, or suns, and now it was the day cycle.

I was lying there, helpless, unable to move, observing the scenery around me — desert and rocks — and then I blacked out again. When I came to, there was a noise and I saw a creature a few yards from me. I could see a creature with four legs and two heads, with two bodies joined together. It leaned over as if to get a better look at me. Then, suddenly, it took off really fast. Later I would figure out that it was a man sitting on top of a horse. I remember he wore a black hat. And it seemed as though he watched me for a long time before he turned and galloped off in such haste.

The day star grew hotter and I kept passing in and out, in and out of consciousness.

My next recollection was that it was again the dark cycle. I could hear noises — machines getting closer — machines roaring and grinding their way up the hillside. Then, the next thing I knew, somebody was picking me up and dragging me by my arms and plopping me onto the ground. My head turned to the side and I looked out of my eye to see that I was up against my four dead crew members. We were all in a row.

The people who came had these crates that were long and rectangular shaped, and they arranged them in a circle around us. I heard several people laughing and somebody kicked me. It was a big creature. They talked in this funny language that I didn't understand. I didn't know what they were saying.

I must have passed out again, because the next thing I remember was being jolted back from out of my body by some cold stuff. I was put into this plastic wrapper and there was cold stuff in it. They picked it up and I was thinking, *What is this? I can't see, and I've got all this cold stuff around me.* Then I was being zippered up, closed inside this bag with the cold stuff surrounding me.

Then I felt myself moving. I was being transported down the winding road or path the machines had come up. When I came to again, I was inside this building. Someone had unzipped the bag I was in and I had a fairly good view of inside the building.

My guide, Khinyeo, appeared then in his astral form. A Zeta Reticulan, he stood before me and made me step outside my body. I hovered in the air inside of this building, which was round. There was a round roof on it, and I could see all these people working around me. It was hot and some of them had removed their shirts. They were busy putting things in piles. Everything was being sorted and catalogued as to size and shape.

"Observe, child," Khinyeo told me. "Pay attention to what you are looking at."

"But, Khinyeo... why?"

He was firm and authoritative. "Because you will remember all of this." Then he led me outside the building and showed me how they were taking metal and equipment in very large boxes and crates and loading them onto vehicles with wheels. Then the vehicles with wheels took the crates to the big silver birds. There were two big silver birds in the distance, and these crates were being loaded onto them.

As I was hovering over the bag with my body packed in the cold medium, someone came over and zipped the bag back up. Then they placed it in a crate with cedar chips or sawdust, and they packed the other four crew members like that, too. On the sides of the crates they had imprinted MUNITIONS or ORDNANCE. They apparently didn't want to arouse suspicion as to the crates' true contents. Then they placed those on the silver bird.

I was able to observe all of this outside my body.

Then Khinyeo made me return to my body. The next thing I remember was being on this cold table after we arrived at our destination. I happened to move my head ever so slightly, and then I heard a bunch of noise. The big creatures dressed in white were shouting and yelling to one another. Soon there were dozens of them surrounding the table I was on. After they removed my uniform and boots, I had tubes shoved up me. Tubes were shoved up my mouth and up my unmentionable places. They began putting stuff on me, trying to check my heart, blood pressure and all that stuff.

Mostly what I remember is that the room didn't smell good. It smelled like death.

My ship was an XBAOTTIG model, a version of a swept-back delta wing design. This vehicle comes in three different models. There's a small design to hold a crew of two. The next is medium sized, designed to hold a crew of four to eight. And there is a larger version, designed to hold a crew of twelve to forty. The swept-back delta wings were created shortly before the horseshoe deltas were phased out, because horseshoe ships were becoming obsolete.

15

A word about my crew: Naylaiu was a xeno biologist, whose job was to collect alien plants and life forms on planets not native to our own solar system.

Shienyah was a linguist, trained to interpret languages into our Kebban dialect.

Lorkiah was a second-in-command, a junior commander in her training to become a pilot.

Kiayha was a navigator and second-in-rank pilot.

About the second ship, it was a large saucer that held twelve scientists, one being my brother Ja-Rod. When my ship went down, she scattered fiber optic cables and hydraulic cords and hundreds of microchips and pieces of long metal strips called *Moinjes*, which are a type of structural beam. There were also devices there in the wreckage that were precursors to your modern picture cell phones. It took several huge crates to contain most of the wreckage and the largest sections that remained intact were packaged in large tarps and flown in huge planes.

2

Stranded

On the third day of September in the year 1958, I was born on Planet Earth in a small town in Ohio. This incarnation on an unfamiliar and somewhat hostile world caused me many problems from the very start. I found out later in life how things were in the beginning from my Native American grandmother, who was half Cherokee and lived in the mountains in the Appalachians. She would tell me things when I had the privilege of visiting her.

Grandmother told me I was special and that I came from the stars. She explained that my father was from the stars and that my mother had conceived me aboard a space ship after she had been abducted. I don't remember much about my Earth parents, because I was removed from their home when I was either 3 or 4. I was told my birth mother was a drug addict and an alcoholic and could no longer take proper care of me. I have no idea why or how they chose my mother. At one time I was told she was "into UFOs," and that she talked to the star people.

At the time of my birth I had a twin brother. He was not as fortunate as I. He was completely blind and deaf — deformed and defective. He was taken away from the start and placed in a home as he was little more than a vegetable. Khinyeo once told me that the first batch of hybrids didn't turn out well. "Some species produce good hybrids and other species do not," he said. Alpha type hybrids were not compatible enough to live on Earth. I was told, "Betas resemble humans, but are Grays." I was part of an experiment. I was from the Beta batch of hybrids. To this day I do not know whether my twin brother still lives or made his transition. It was never discussed. I was placed in several different foster homes as a young child. And then, around age 6 or 7, I went to the home of Mr. and Mrs. Riley (not their real name). Their foster home was out in the country. I will not reveal the true names of these foster parents because of the awful things that happened to me while I lived with them. Mr. Riley would abuse me while Mrs. Riley was at work, and the both of them were very strict with me at all times. I was denied from the start a "normal" childhood.

Mr. Riley was a retired military officer. I believe he was Air Force, but I didn't know at the time. I only know that their home was selected for me to stay in because my birth mother talked and someone found out that she claimed to have gotten pregnant when she was aboard a space craft. Apparently someone took her seriously enough to mention it to the authorities.

One of my earliest recollections is when I was in my crib and my Earth family was passed out on the bed. I now believe they were in suspended animation or an induced trance state. They were silent and didn't move, and I grew frightened.

Then this little man came into the room. I was not at all afraid of him. He looked at me and he said, "That man on the bed is not your father."

It was just as though I knew this little man. And indeed I had known him from my past life as I discovered later. He was small with great big shiny black eyes that looked wet. His skin was soft, almost a suede-like material, and he wore a tight-fitting uniform which appeared silky and was one piece. There were no buttons or zippers.

The little man picked me up out of my crib and he had very long fingers. He had to use his mind to pick me up, because physically he was quite weak. By using his mental powers, he could more easily lift me. He called me "Sanni."

Next, I remember being taken to a really big white room. There were all these so-called "Martians" there, as well as other children who were about my age or a little bit older. The "Martians" were Grays, Insectoids that were Mantis-like, and they interacted with us physically using toys. Later I was to find out this was the nursery aboard the mother ship.

On this and during subsequent visits, we were told that we had to use our minds. We sat in a big circle and didn't have any clothes on. Half of us were hybrids and half were human children. We would use our minds to make a silver ball move across the floor, or they would take one hybrid child and match him or her with a human child, and they would test us. They would give us a symbol and we would have to figure out what that symbol meant, all by telepathy. We weren't allowed to gesture with our hands or speak.

Communication was always through the mind. When the little man first picked me up out of my crib, I automatically talked with him using my mind. I did not use my voice. If you are wondering what that is like, imagine hearing the language in your head. They didn't speak in English. Yet I knew their language. And the man told me that when I got a little older, my memories would come back.

There were many night-time visits while I was very young. Sometimes I had visits during the daytime. I was never afraid of them. I felt as if I knew them from somewhere. A ball of light would come into my bedroom and I would hear a being say in my mind, "Do you want to play? I've got toys for you to play with," or "It's play time!" or "The Martians are coming," or something similar to that.

They would take me out of the room in a beam of light. It would be as if I were floating or flying, because I would have these dreams where I believed I was flying, but now I don't think they were dreams. I would go with them, in the beam of light, and onto the round thing — the great big house in the sky as I referred to it — and when I got older I knew it was a space ship.

From a very young age I started having weird flashbacks. I would see fleeting images of myself sitting at a console, and there would be four other people and they were all dressed in silver flight suits. I was operating a machine that could pass for a computer, but they didn't have computers like that on this planet at that time. I was on board a vessel of some sort, almost like the cockpit of an airplane, and yet it was too sophisticated to be an airplane.

During thunderstorms I began feeling as if I was actually there in the flashbacks. The first began happening to me when I was 4 years old. I would get upset and scared, and I'd want to tell them, but this voice would pop into my head and say, "No! They would not understand!"

My foster families did not quite know what to think of me as I got older and the flashbacks grew more intense. Then I started getting symbols along with these flashbacks. And one day — I must have been 7 or 8 — I was sitting down and watching the television in the living room when a great big beam of light hit. A bolt of lightning hit outside in the front yard and struck a tree, and it triggered a very intense flashback.

In that flashback I saw that it was dark and raining, and there was huge explosion in the air. The next thing I knew, I saw myself sitting on the wet ground with four other injured people crying out in pain. And then the noise stopped.

The memories continued up to the present time. Lightning storms no longer bother me as much now, unless they are really intense, but I used to get extremely upset every time there was a storm and I'd get those flashbacks.

Around age 6 or 7, I realized I was experiencing a past life. In grade school I kept writing in symbols and the teachers didn't understand the symbols. They would ask, "What are these symbols? Where are you getting these symbols from?"

I would say to them, "That is not for you to know."

I was 12 or 13 before I learned to tell time. It was something I simply couldn't do. Every time I would try to learn how to tell time, I would get communication from that little man and he would say to me, "Time is not in our concepts. We have no concept of time. That is an Earth concept, an artificial means of controlling the world around you, and nature as well. That is not our way!"

The little man said he had known me for a long time and that he also knew my mother and my grandmother. When I asked him his name, he said, "My name is Khinyeo."

Khinyeo would come mostly at night, and whenever he sensed I was in some kind of trouble. He could sense it telepathically. I would often get into trouble around Mr. and Mrs. Riley, and Khinyeo would come to me telepathically and give me signs.

For instance, I might be watching television and he would come to me and say, "I'd like you to go to the window," or "I'd like you to go outside." I would then find an excuse to sneak outside, and when I was outside I would see things up in the sky — UFOs. At that time I referred to them as funny or strange birds, but it was as though I knew them from somewhere.

And as the flashbacks continued while I got older, I came to realize I had been on these birds many, many times, and that I had operated one of these birds — as its pilot.

I was afraid to discuss the visits with my foster parents. I tried it once and only got yelled at and accused of having a wild imagination.

All in all, I lived with about twelve foster families, after I left the Rileys. I stayed with Mr. and Mrs. Riley the longest time — until I was 18 or 19 years old. I can remember a photograph taken of me in a field when I was about 6 or 7, and there was a bunch of other foster children with me. After I came to live with Mr. and Mrs. Riley, they quit taking any more foster children. For some reason they weren't allowed to obtain any more, and I never understood why.

Mr. and Mrs. Riley had kept children for the state. Over the years they must have had about sixty kids, and they received about $500 to $600 per child. Mr. Riley was retired and stayed home, but Mrs. Riley worked during the day as a cook in a school cafeteria. There was a lot of abuse with the other kids, too — not just with me.

In the military Mr. Riley had been something special. He would often say to me, "I know more about you than you can ever imagine." And when he said that, I would have another flashback. I would see myself lying on a steel table with all these people around me. I felt I was gravely injured and that they didn't know how to treat me, and I was trying to talk to them, mind to mind, but I couldn't understand their language and they couldn't communicate the way I could.

The possibility crossed my mind many times, years later, that Mr. Riley had been at Roswell in July 1947.

Once, when I was a teenager, I remember sneaking into Mr. Riley's bedroom and finding his black book. I opened this black book and was looking at it. In it there were photographs and I recognized the being in some of the photographs. They were black-and-white photographs of a being lying on a table, and as I looked at the pictures I began getting more flashbacks. I could even feel the physical pain.

Mr. Riley never found out that I had gotten into that black book. I put the book back in the exact location I had found it.

When I was little, I was afraid of the moon because it used to land in our front yard. I was 5 years old when this happened. In reality, it wasn't the moon but a craft all lit up. Later I learned it was my people visiting me in their "flying house" in the sky.

There was another incident when I was 10 years old and sitting in the apple orchard. It was a nice sunny day, partly cloudy, in late summer or early fall. The apples were getting ripe. I heard a humming noise, like a swarm of bees, and kept looking all over into the woods and there I saw a huge cloud with a disc perched halfway in the cloud. The disc was tilted so that you could see the underside of its hull, and its rim rotated. The object was silver and reflected the sunlight. Suddenly it went sideways and then disappeared.

The next day I remember digging around a tree in the orchard that had huge apples, and finding that the soil around the tree was pitch black. I dug around other trees and the soil was a light brown color. While digging around the tree with the black soil, I hit something hard and discovered two perfectly white round stones that were about the size of tennis balls. They sweated when you held them, and when I dropped them, they didn't break but rolled on their own. They were ceramic-like in texture and had pock marks all over them.

3

The Social Workers

During my childhood the beings that visited me were more than guides. I have called them guides. They would leave things for me in the yard or on the property, and then Mr. Riley would find them and confiscate them. I'm talking about objects such as glowing metallic balls with these rods where, if you hold them just right, they will hum. And they were magnetic.

I once acquired from the beings an object that was volleyball size and covered with spikes. It was white with rainbow colors all over it — iridescent in color. It had long spikes and would move on its own across the cement. I remember leaving it lie there in the long grass, and Mr. Riley hit it with his lawn mower. It made a funny noise and then turned into this really long strip that was about half an inch across, and then the spikes laid down on top of one another, overlapping.

The "toy" ended up in a great big cardboard box in the Rileys' basement, along with similar objects. The social workers would take these artifacts with them whenever they would visit.

Another night-time event I had as a child was the time I woke up cold and turned over to pull the blankets up over me. I discovered my hands were wet, which woke me up. Then I found out I was in our field and my pajamas were turned inside out. I could smell a smoky odor. I looked in the direction of the odor and saw a big circle, black in color. I know I did not sleepwalk. I was 8 years old when that experience happened.

Every two or three months, while I was staying with Mr. and Mrs. Riley, social workers would come to visit. These people seemed extremely interested in me. They would arrive in dark blue vans and they wore dark blue uniforms that were almost black. The women social workers wore hats and would wear a jacket with a matching skirt, with shoes that matched, and a light blue blouse with some kind of insignia on it.

The visits were always planned. Sometimes there were men social workers. They were usually older, white-haired men. Two or three people would come at a time. Mr. and Mrs. Riley were always there when the social workers came. They were not interested in any of the other foster children.

I remember the social workers would ask Mr. and Mrs. Riley, "How is it doing?" "What kind of food does it eat?" They always referred to me as "it." They never referred to me by name. I would climb on the man's lap and pick at his pretty eagles and star things on his jacket.

Once a year I would have to get into one of the blue vans and sit real close between two women. Then I would be taken to a facility that was far away. We would arrive within a day and we would make stops to meet other vehicles on the way.

I can remember one of the women saying to me once, "Now, you be a good little thing and we'll get you some candy," or else they would promise me a toy if I behaved. They were very cold and business-like.

In later years I was taken to another place. It would take us two or three days and nights to get there. I remember that the place was really dry and there weren't a lot trees. It was somewhere in the Western United States.

At the earlier place, I saw a lot of airplanes. It was like a huge airport. We had to go through a lot of gates and checkpoints. Everybody was dressed almost identically. There were no other children, although in one instance I saw another person in there who was fairly small for an adult and we spoke mind to mind. I remember that when I got to this place, we went through a long tunnel — a really long tunnel — and it was weird because, when I got older, it reminded me of a factory.

The hospital room I stayed in was strange. There were no pictures on the walls, just sophisticated machines and two or three people who stood there, wearing uniforms and holding guns with straps on them. These men wore hats with their uniforms. One would stand next to the door of my room and one would sit.

Tests were run on me at the Eastern facility. Then someone would come in and show me pictures and say, "You know what this is? You tell us how it operates." And they would hold a black box and they would give me an identical black box, as if we were able to talk mind to mind through the boxes. They showed me pictures that were of propulsion units for rockets and similar things.

When I got older, during one of those visits to the facility that was in the desert, I was taken by some people who wore white coats onto the floor of the factory, as I called it, where everybody wore white jackets, white pants, white hats and white shoes. They said to me, "Tell us how these operate, because we know you know how these operate, and we know you were involved with these."

And as long as I had that black box in my possession, I would communicate and say, "That one there operates by antimatter." So, I actually knew the information that they wanted. Even though I was in a child's body, they talked to me as though I were an adult and I was able to give them the information they wanted. Sometimes they used a prod that would shock me. I remember this little man with a goatee and glasses who was very interested in astronomy.

They would reward me by showing me movies. The films would show the sky and there would be lights flying across the sky being tracked by radar. I knew what those things were.

Khinyeo told me these people were trying to get information from our people so that they could use the information against us. I am quite sure that Khinyeo prevented me from giving them too much information.

One time when I went to that desert facility, a man came up to me and asked, "Do you recognize this?" And he showed me a long piece of metal. He actually let me hold it. It had symbols on it. He said, "You do recall this? You do recognize this?" And I thought, oh my goodness, these are the very symbols that I write! Naturally they had taken samples of my writing earlier. The piece of metal was part of the wreckage from my spaceship.

In grade school I started writing the symbols. I would pick up a pencil and start getting images. Then I would draw the images that came to me — one after another. When I made these symbols I would have flashbacks of being on that vehicle with the four other people, with me operating the computer, and those symbols would come up on the computer screen.

I was told by the people at the facility about my symbols, "Of all the hundreds or more languages, there are none that come close to this. This is no known alphabet." Well, certainly not on your planet. The symbols are from my home world.

When the black box was held up to me, these people could communicate and they would say very technical things to me. Many times they asked me to tell them what the symbols meant. I allowed a few of them to be deciphered, but most of them I withheld the information. Khinyeo would appear and say, "No, child, they would use that against us. If they find that out, it will unlock the key to advancing their technology, and they are not ready for that." It was as though some of the symbols completed a formula. I could not understand why they wanted all the samples of skin, hair and blood that they took from me. They also tested my mind. They did all kinds of tests on me. They would even test my reaction to food. They would hold out all kinds of different foods and study my reactions. I often wondered if regular children went through the same things that I did.

My intelligence was tested and I scored way above other kids my age. All the time that I attended school while living with Mr. and Mrs. Riley, I was not allowed to make friends. I was put into special education classes and labeled as mentally retarded. I don't know how they came up with that when my intelligence was ranked so high. I guess the reason I was placed in special education was because of my difficulty with the concept of time and not understanding how to use money.

Social workers often appeared at my school, the same ones that would visit our house and take me on the yearly expeditions to the facilities. The teachers weren't allowed to get friendly with me. They weren't allowed to even interact with me beyond a simple level. The social workers saw to that.

Most of the kids in school shunned me. I remember when I'd get on the school bus, there were plenty of seats, but the other kids would place their books down on the seat next to them so that I couldn't sit there beside them. I always perceived myself as being different from others. One night, during an event, I confronted Khinyeo with this problem and demanded, "Why is it that everybody shuns me when I don't do a thing to make people want to avoid me?"

He said, "Child, it is because you are not from here."

One day in grade school the class was sent outside. We were doing a lesson on weather. While we were outside and the teacher was talking about the sun, I suddenly blurted out, "You're not supposed to have just one sun. You're supposed to have two!"

The teacher looked at me, shocked, and ran back into the classroom. I heard her tell someone, "You'd better call the social worker!"

An event occurred at school real early one morning, when I was in either the third or fourth grade. The teacher had just pulled the curtains open at the windows. She looked outside and then called everyone over to look at "the funny airplane."

I was one of the first students to get to the window. When the other kids got there, they began to cry and yell. I couldn't figure out why. What I saw seemed to be the most beautiful thing. It was just incredible! The object in the sky resembled

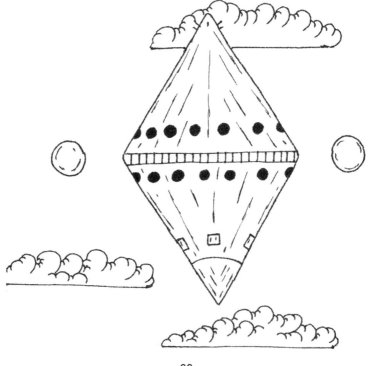

two cones with their points at either end. It had a silvery color and a row of windows on the upper section and bottom section. The object rotated and didn't make a sound. On each side of it there were two balls made of the same material. These were not attached, but you could see that all three of these objects were rotating at the same time.

As I watched it, the sun reflected off the windows on it, and I felt this great sense of peace come over me. I felt like I was communicating with the object. This seemed to go on for a very long time, and then, all of a sudden, all three of the objects simply shot straight upwards and disappeared.

There was another incident that occurred during my school years, when I was on a school bus. I was going home and, normally, the school bus was noisy. But this time it was as though all the kids were "turned off." You couldn't hear a thing. The driver just kept driving straight ahead as if nothing were wrong.

All of a sudden, I put my books down and I had this strong urge to look out the window. Over in the field that we were passing — I don't know how many feet away it was — there was this great big round, metallic, silvery object hovering over the field. I could not take my eyes off it. I don't think anyone else on the bus was allowed to see it.

Another incident happened once during recess time. This was in fifth grade, and all the kids were outside playing. Suddenly, the sun just blocked out and all was dark. It was as though all the other kids had run away. It grew quiet. I looked up and saw a dark object come over me. It hovered in the air, this great big round object that was several feet up in the air — maybe 20, 30 or 40 feet. And I felt these vibrations coming from it.

I don't know what happened next, but suddenly I was sitting back in the classroom, half asleep, and I didn't know how I had gotten into the chair. Nobody seemed to remember anything about the incident.

There was another daylight event at school. Again it was recess time, and I had the urge to sneak around the playground over to where there was a nearby woods. I sneaked off into the woods and found this strange insect. It was a beautiful emerald green praying mantis. I remember how it was sticking up and I was so fascinated by him.

The next thing I knew, I was in a mist — a white mist that surrounded me. The mantis was gone and there were three of those people that resembled the little man who had picked me up as a baby and told me he was my father. I went with these people, inside a machine that was hidden in the woods, and I saw something on that machine that made me have flashbacks. I saw the exact computer and console that I had often seen in my flashbacks.

Khinyeo said to me, "You were here before you took this form." Then he added, "You caused an accident to happen. When you get older, I will explain it to you."

Later I would discover that in that other life I had disobeyed orders not to lead an expedition to this planet, because Earth is a very aggressive, war-like planet that could bring about its own destruction if it isn't careful.

In that life, as well as in this one, I was fascinated by Earth's animals and all the life you have here. How beautiful this Earth is! As a scientist, I found it thrilling to collect living things and study them. The temptation to disobey orders and come to Earth anyway was too strong for me.

I was a lieutenant, much like a commander, in that former life. The others had agreed to come with me because they knew they would not be allowed to come here anymore and, like me, they wanted to observe and collect specimens. But I was held accountable more than the others.

I feel that the flashbacks I had, and the message from Khinyeo telling me that I must remember who I am and that I should not forget what I am, were important for me to know at an early age.

After the crash at Roswell in July 1947, I survived approximately one month in your Earth time. I was kept at a facility similar to the one I was taken to as a child in this lifetime. It was some big place in the Eastern United States. I was in extreme pain and my inside parts were severely burned. My right side was hurt and burned. I lay on a steel table, stripped of my uniform and exposed.

They didn't know what to do for me, or what to give me to relieve the pain. There wasn't anything they could do for me, but they interrogated me. Sometimes when I would go back to that facility as a child, they would show me things that I remembered from that past life, such as the black boxes and other small machines and devices.

After that life ended, I can remember not being in a body, just being a form of energy and flying around. It is hard to describe this. I could see everything and I could experience things without being in a body.

I suppose one reason I was doing all the wandering was because I was trying to find where my ship had gone down. I would call out to Khinyeo, "I want to go back to my ship!" But he would say, "No, you can't!" I could have been tracked and reported as a UFO while I was a ball of energy.

The plan implemented by the Council and Khinyeo was that I should reincarnate on Earth as a hybrid, in order for their message to get through. The Earth has to know why we have been visiting them, and they have to know that we have been visiting them more than just a few decades.

I have come back as a hybrid in order to teach others and to bring awareness. Your planet, Earth, has been visited by others for millions of years. Khinyeo said I was part of all that. I can remember real vivid flashbacks of being over a desert in a circular ship with a squadron of maybe five or half a dozen other ships flying over the pyramids. I can remember one or two of our ships landing in the vast desert and talking to the Egyptians.

My race is Essassani. The star system I came from is Zeta Reticuli. The lifespan of a Zeti is longer than that of a person on Earth. A 90-year-old Zetan would be considered on Earth just out of their teens. Our civilization was in existence even before your Earth was formed.

Because I was different, I didn't get along with humans in my childhood. The other children ridiculed and teased me. I suppose they were scared of me, because I wasn't one of them, and because I wrote in strange symbols and I had visits.

When I got older, the school kids used to bring up the incident about the "funny airplane" and they associated me with the funny airplane. They used to call me "Martian" in school.

Even when I was in college, I remember being in a computer course and two of the students remembered me from grade school. "There's Martian," he told his friend. "She went in a flying saucer. Do you remember the funny airplane back in third grade?"

And my thought was, "Oh, no, don't tell me they're here..."

I wanted to fit in as a human, but Khinyeo would say, "Child, you cannot. You cannot fully blend in." That was due to the fact that I am wired as a Zeti in my thinking so as not to lose my connection to my ET heritage from being a hybrid.

As mentioned before, when I stayed with the Rileys, social workers in dark navy uniforms with light blue shirts and blouses would visit me about once a month and I was referred to as an "it." Finally, at the age of 19, the social workers decided it was time that I left the home of Mr. and Mrs. Riley. I was put into another military home. Most of my foster homes had been military families. Once I got to a certain age, the visits to the facilities each year stopped.

Yet in a way I feel they are still keeping track of me. Every time I see a person wearing a uniform, I get uptight, sometimes even have anxiety attacks.

In the next home, which was a group home, I met Jim, whom the owners assigned to manage their group home when they weren't around or out of town. Jim was out of the military and he used to run the home like a camp, making everyone get up and work at certain times.

Jim never showed interest in the two retarded ladies at that home, but he showed an interest in me that made me very uncomfortable. Jim used to drink and take drugs on top of alcohol. My bedroom was across from his master bedroom at the group home. Jim used to come into my room at night and fondle me and demand I meet his insatiable sex appetite. To me sex is very painful. Jim once threatened to use a scissors on me down there — and did cut me — to make me larger like Earth females, to accept his member.

I was terrified of him as he told me he was labeled a psychotic. His wife and six daughters were hurt badly once when he tried to commit suicide by driving his car with them in it into a large tree many years ago.

Several times other residents would go home to their families for weekends, but I was forced to stay there at that house with him and wear very short skirts and act like a whore to him. This goes against my people's morals as a Zeti and is an evil on Earth, in my opinion.

I'd have to respond to everything he made me say and do. Jim was very manipulative toward me and used mind control on me to make me obey him without question. He used to deprive me of sleep and then would lock me up in a tiny room with no light or else have light on constantly. He'd play loud music non-stop and make me take drugs against my will.

Jim used to interrogate me in a room with only two chairs and a small table. On that table was a loaded gun that he would point at me if I didn't answer him to suit him. He claimed to know everything about me and how he got this information I don't know, nor do I ever wish to.

He used to have a redbone hound that he would force to do nasty things to my body when he would get drunk, and he'd hold that gun on me to make sure I behaved.

After I stayed there with him awhile, I went to his mom's farm in the country. His mom had about seven heart attacks. It was at this farm where the rape at gunpoint occurred in 1977. Also, Jim would stand over my bed holding a large knife over me and I caught him two times because he awakened me. He used to sleepwalk a lot. I now have a fear of anyone with a knife or if they are close by and pick up a knife I have panic attacks.

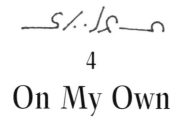

4

On My Own

Several years passed after I finished high school. I then decided to go to college. I was hoping I could better this world and share my knowledge. I went to a four-year college in the East where I wanted to get an associate of arts degree. Then later I attended a special college for mortuary science. I had the idea that if I could be a mortician, I could use my art skills in restorative techniques.

That experience ended abruptly. One day while I was in the clinical laboratory, I saw apparitions. They were of two young people who had been killed in a motorcycle accident. Their spirits were in the room because they didn't want to leave their bodies.

Khinyeo came to me and said, "It's time to leave. You cannot be in this field. Besides, your gifts will be awakened soon."

I had always been able to see things before they happened — premonitions — and I would sometimes know by intuition when someone was going to get sick. I would often tell my foster parents when someone was going to have a stroke or a heart attack, and then it would occur. I could walk into a room at times and have the clock stop or go backwards. One time, at Thanksgiving, they had me set the good silverware out on the table, and later they demanded to know how it had all gotten bent. I had the ability of mind over matter when I was very young. But those abilities got turned off, for the most part, due to the mind control and psychotropic drugs that were used to brainwash me at the facilities.

It wasn't too long after the experience with the apparitions at the mortuary college when I was sitting in the city park and got hit by a car. The driver was doing drugs and there was a drive-by shooting. The driver lost control of the car and it hit me.

That's when my life changed. That's when my psychic gifts, which had been mostly dormant since birth, were switched back on.

I met Stanley shortly before I attended college. We met in a New Age bookstore at Thanksgiving time. He was looking at books on UFOs and I was drawn to that area, for some reason. We got to talking and he finally said to me, "You're not from here."

I said, "I know that. I come from a place that has a double sun."

Stanley recognized that place. But he wasn't allowed to have all of his memories. Stanley had a deep interest in ufology and believed in other worlds that had life. He had blue eyes and was almost completely bald. He was tall and thin and had big hands. He wore glasses and was Jewish.

We agreed to meet again and talk. The second time we met at a video game place, and after that we agreed to meet each other for lunch every other day. Stanley had a wonderful smile. He had a soft voice and was an avid reader. He collected books, mostly about different countries on Earth and geography.

The accident in the park left me partially blind in one eye and deaf in one ear. It also injured my back. I had been able to work at various jobs before the accident. I used to do collating, sorting and small machine operation in factories.

Most of those jobs came through agencies, but one of them I had actually applied for the way most people do.

When I met Stanley I was in my 20s. He was in his 50s. He had such a gentle temperament. We rarely had any arguments or fights. Like me, Stanley had a sensitive stomach and couldn't handle stress well, so when there were differences we talked things out in a peaceful way and never jumped down each other's throats over things.

We knew each other for twelve years. During that time we did things together and had a relationship, although it was not the usual man-woman relationship others on your planet experience. We often kissed and held each other, but we never had sexual intercourse. He understood it was too painful for me, so we found other ways to express our love for each other.

One of my most memorable experiences was when I was in college and Stanley sat in class with me for a day in order to give me support. Many times we took the bus to nearby cities on day trips. He remembered special events and treated me as if I were the most special thing to him. Stanley was a wonderful companion to me.

And then Stanley got sick and he refused to seek treatment. I first noticed he was ill when he had a change in eating habits. He went from being a hearty eater to eating only salads, and finally drinking only water and living on Tums and Rolaids. He began to lose weight and became very shaky. His energy level changed from being active to just lying around all day. He wouldn't go to doctors. He'd had a previous cancer that had gone into remission years ago, but it apparently returned.

One time when I was with Stanley, we were listening to a song on the radio and Stanley said to me, "Oh, I really like that song." It was John Denver singing *Colorado Rocky Mountain High*. I turned to Stanley and said, "Stanley, I'm going there someday."

John Denver is one of my spirit guides. It is an interesting coincidence that John Denver was born in Roswell, New Mexico, and that all of my life I have been drawn to Roswell.

It's a wonder that Mr. and Mrs. Riley even let me listen to John Denver music. When I lived with them all those years, everything I saw on television or read was censored. I was forbidden to watch anything about outer space. All science fiction was denied me. Every Wednesday Mr. and Mrs. Riley would go to the bowling alley, so I'd sneak downstairs and turn on the television to watch *Star Trek*. I knew what channel the program was on without having to look at the TV Guide. *Star Trek* fascinated me and I could identify with one of the characters.

Mr. and Mrs. Riley also forbid me from watching nature shows, something I have never been able to understand.

I suppose it's also a wonder I was ever allowed to visit my Cherokee grandmother. She was a little woman with long hair who believed in the traditional ways. She lived in a woods with surrounding mountains, in one of the Carolinas. I received letters from her once in a while, but Mr. and Mrs. Riley would open them up and read them before they gave them to me. I had to be very, very good in order to earn the privilege to visit my grandmother, and I would travel by bus. I was able to visit my grandmother once a year.

I would stay about a week. She used to talk about the star people all the time. I remember she had animal hides up on the walls, along with antlers and feathers, and she had many aquariums and books. She also had several cats and a dog or two whenever I visited. She would set me on her lap and show me a scrapbook. She would show me objects, the same ones I had seen — namely unidentified flying objects, or UFOs.

Grandmother told me I was special because part of me was from the stars. She kept saying that the humans shot some of my people down in 1947. She said a little man visited her when she was younger and told her I would come.

My grandmother was in her 90s when she left this dimension. One of the last things she ever said to me was that I would someday be on the "bird," the big silver round bird.

It was Thanksgiving Day and I was on my way over to Stanley's apartment. We were going to spend the day together. That morning Khinyeo had come to me and said, "You must be strong. Something has happened and you are going to get upset, but it's imperative that you stay calm and do all that you are supposed to do. Is that clear?"

"What, Khinyeo?" I had asked. "What's going to happen? What are you talking about?"

He wouldn't tell me. "Just be strong, child. Stay calm. Do what you need to do."

I had a key to Stanley's apartment and decided to let myself in. I noticed there were two newspapers left outside his door, which was unusual because Stanley loved to read his newspaper every day, and sometimes we would read them together.

I let myself into the apartment. Things were strangely quiet. Too quiet. And all of the curtains were closed, which was strange. Then I saw a translucent black orb that was approximately 4 feet in diameter suspended in the middle of the living room, about two or three feet from the floor. It slowly moved over to the couch and then it disappeared with a loud pop as I was watching. It sounded very much like a balloon when it pops.

The apartment was extremely cold, for some reason. Stanley didn't answer when I called out his name.

When I walked into his bedroom, there he was, lying on

his back on the bed. He had left his body. It was quite a shock to me, seeing Stanley dead. He had vomited blood everywhere. I was traumatized, yet remembered what Khinyeo had said to me earlier: "You must be strong. Stay calm and do what you need to do..."

Because I believed so much in my father, I was able to pick up the telephone and call the police, then the mortuary and members of Stanley's family, and handle all the details that followed without once falling apart. Later, after everything was taken care of, I fell apart and cried hysterically over Stanley.

For a long time I grieved his passing. Why had he left me? Why couldn't I have a lifetime companion to be with during my stay on Earth? I wanted to leave the planet and go back to my ship! I didn't want to stay here on this hostile world another day.

At times when I'd be drowning in my self pity, Khinyeo would come to me and say, "You must complete your mission before you are allowed to return to us."

"What mission?" I'd demand to know.

"Your penance," he'd reply. "You must pay for what you did — crashing your ship and killing not only four of your companions who were on board, but also the twelve astronauts on board the ship that was behind you!"

"What must I do, Father? What *is* my mission?"

Khinyeo would say, "You are to teach about your home world and how things can be different on planet Earth. You must spread the word that we have been visiting their world for a long, long time, and that there is another way other than war, destruction and greed!"

"Is there anything else?"

"Yes, child. You must return to the crash site in the desert. Eventually you must relocate to that area on the planet that is known as New Mexico."

That seemed almost impossible. How could I possibly get to the Southwest? I had no money. I had no means. I couldn't drive. Who would help me get to Roswell? And what did Khinyeo mean I would eventually need to relocate to New Mexico?

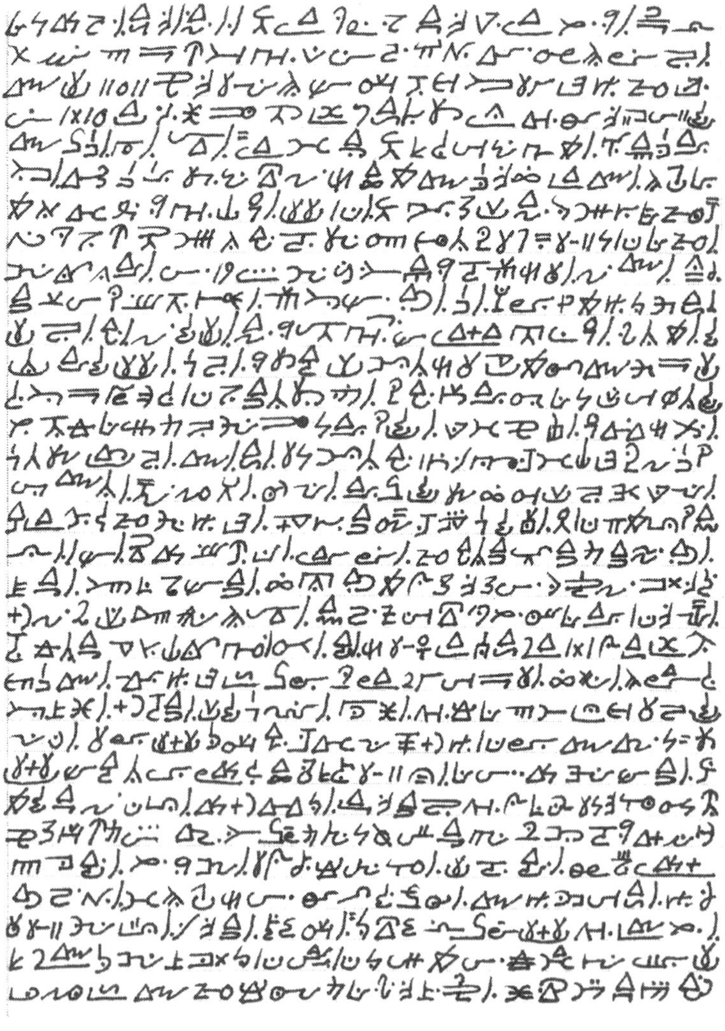

A sample of my writing

5

The Difficult Years

After Stanley left this dimension, I was alone in a big city in the Eastern United States. I prefer not to name the place, because I feel there are enough big cities like it and it could be anywhere in the United States.

Everyday life for me was a boring routine of getting up in the morning, making my instant coffee, and listening to the morning news on television. Around eleven o'clock — or sometimes not until four o'clock — I would go downstairs to check my mailbox, and sometimes I'd walk over to the Kroger store, which was in a high crime neighborhood with lots of drugs and violence.

I lived in a government-subsidized apartment in a low-income neighborhood. There were constant sirens and trains passed by about every ten minutes. My apartment building housed mostly elderly people, many of whom were ill. There were not a lot of young people. There was no one in their 30s except me.

The people around me seemed to have nothing better to do than to snoop in everyone's business. They gossiped a lot and I didn't talk to many people as I didn't want to get involved in their energies. I always knew when a person died because I could see their apparition in the hallways or in the laundry room or somewhere else around.

There was a huge duck pond outside the apartment building. I used to feed the ducks, until someone shot one with an arrow. After that I no longer had any desire to feed the ducks and left them alone.

Once in a while I would ride the metro bus downtown, which was an all afternoon event. I'd go to the library, where I'd use the computers and check out books. The buses were not a pleasant means of transportation, they were always crowded, but they were the only means I had.

The apartment building got locked up each night at six-thirty, due to the high crime neighborhood, and people kept their apartment doors locked at all times. The hallways were so close together that you could hear everyone's TV and their conversations.

Once in a while I liked to put jigsaw puzzles together with a few of the people whom I made friends with.

I heard about a group that had started up, a support group for abductees. My father, Khinyeo, advised me to go and help educate the humans there. A lot of them didn't accept me or want to hear what I had to say, however. But it was at one of those support group meetings when a man gave me a sample copy of a publication known as *The Star Beacon*. I had never seen a copy of it before. I read it and loved it.

The Star Beacon was full of articles that talked about space, and there were letters from people who'd had contact or abduction experiences. I couldn't put it down. I decided to take some money out and subscribe to this monthly UFO newsletter. Little did I know at the time that by taking that one step, I was reaching out for my goal of relocating to the Southwest.

Then I found out *The Star Beacon* had just begun a Galaxy Wide Friendship Club. I immediately joined the Friendship Club, in hopes of meeting others like me who weren't from this world. It cost just ten dollars for a lifetime membership.

I got replies from other members in the pen pal club,

some who were curious about me, and others who were not very kind. A few were extremely skeptical of my claim to be who I was, even though they themselves claimed to have known people such as I on this Earth. They claimed to believe in the same things that I did, yet criticized me and thought I was a joke.

Being Zeta Reticulan, I was misjudged by people who believed the Gray race was all bad. I knew all my life that I was different and had longed to meet others like me. A much more advanced civilization can pass off their people as indigenous inhabitants to any planet they are assigned to while on a mission to observe and monitor another world.

One of the members of the Friendship Club, a younger man from a foreign country, acted as if he knew everything and claimed to have seen ships, and yet he refused to believe in my reality. In fact, he was downright mean in his letters to me, accusing me of being a fake, telling me I had to be making all of this up so that I'd receive attention.

He had me so riled and upset that I telephoned Ann Ulrich, the publisher of *The Star Beacon*, who had started the Galaxy Wide Friendship Club. Ann lived in Colorado and I was lucky enough to reach her at home. I remember I was crying and very emotional when I told her what the man had written.

I have honestly believed everything my Zeti people have told me, that I'm a hybrid, and that I was sent to help Earth and to fulfill my mission to connect with my past in 1947. I told Ann that some of those people I wrote or talked to said they were open-minded light workers, yet they were closed-minded to the idea of others living on Earth who are not from this planet. I should think a true light worker would be open-minded toward others not from their world and accept their reality.

Khinyeo told me I wasn't to write to those who criticized

me. In fact, Khinyeo wanted to abduct a few of those who had rejected me, but the Council told him no. They told him those people will eventually find out for themselves that there are beings like me on Earth. Someday, Khinyeo explained to me, those people will have their minds opened, but it will be by the Council. All Zetis are shape shifters and have to assume the form of the inhabitants of the world they are assigned to monitor. Yet they continue to have traits that set them apart from the natives. Not all E.T.s resemble the product of Hollywood!

According to my father, Khinyeo, most humans are blind to the fact that hybrids and E.T.s exist on this planet, because of society's conditioning them to not believe in life on other worlds. A person could see a ship overhead and deny it is real, because his or her programming has told them it's an illusion or a trick and they didn't really see anything.

But there are others like me scattered around on Earth, but who must remain in the closet, so to speak, about their heritage. There are probably half a dozen to a hundred Zetis. They remain closeted because of the rejection and ridicule from society, and because of the mistaken idea that UFOs aren't real, part of the government's coverup. Most people cannot imagine how hard it is trying to fit into human society when you are not native.

Of course, not everyone in the Friendship Club ridiculed me. For instance, I met my dear friend Irene through *The Star Beacon*. Ours evolved into a wonderful friendship. She had absolutely no trouble accepting me for who I am. I wrote to some of the other members, but Khinyeo didn't want me writing to a lot of them. Zetis aren't used to emotions and we often have trouble handling our emotions. Emotions cause hurt and pain.

I liked Ann's energy and was thrilled with her newsletter.

When I called her to tell her how some of the members were ridiculing me in the Friendship Club, she listened and comforted me. We shared letters back and forth, and I wondered what it was like in Colorado. Did Ann live way up in the mountains like my favorite singer, John Denver?

For years I had wanted to see Colorado and visit the place where John Denver lived. I told Ann about my desire to visit Colorado, and she suggested that I visit her sometime. In *The Star Beacon* I had read about many others whose experiences were similar to mine, although not just like mine. I felt that by visiting Ann in Colorado, I might get a chance to meet others like me.

Ann told me she wanted to print my story in her newsletter and include some of my art work. I agreed, and in April 1999 Ann published "Stranded on Earth: The Plight of Sanni" in *The Star Beacon*. The issue also included a message from my species to the people of Earth.

Meanwhile, the city I lived in was affecting my physical health. My lifestyle was very mundane. The housing complex I lived in was run by a Jewish organization. Years before, when I had known Stanley, I had more or less embraced his religion, Judaism, and had even changed my name to a Jewish name.

Due to the accident years ago, when the car had hit me in the park, I could hardly walk. Not only was my back injured, but the accident left me blind in one eye and deaf in one ear. Some days I could hardly even go to the elevator because my back would hurt me so much. The humidity didn't help either. Urban life was miserable with hot, humid summers and cold, damp winters. There was always pollution and noise. People weren't good about keeping their sidewalks shoveled. People weren't friendly toward me, especially because I looked poor and handicapped. They were quick to put judgment labels on me. They were cold-hearted as if I were a bum.

My lifestyle was not a healthy one. Living for years with the elderly and the sick in that housing complex made me look and feel old myself. I wasn't even 40, yet I could easily pass as a decrepit old woman, at least from a distance. I had nothing to do except stay at home much of the time and watch TV and listen to my neighbors complain about their aches and pains.

Most of the time I had very little energy or enthusiasm. It was all I could do to get by day after day. I had my two cats, Kitty Girl and E.T., to take care of, and they were good company. Sometimes I worked on sewing my life-like E.T. dolls. I started making the dolls so that I have replicas of my people. First I made one of my father, Khinyeo. He sleeps with me at night and is a source of great comfort to me.

I was considered odd by the neighbors because I burned incense in my apartment and I could see their auras. They didn't understand why I had crystals scattered all over my rooms. Most of them avoided me like the plague. Once in a while I would help the apartment manager with some office work, by filing maintenance reports or doing a little mailing, and she said I was a good worker. In exchange, she'd let me use the office photocopier to make copies of my art work.

Finally, in the spring of 2000, Ann Ulrich announced that she and her soul mate, Starhawk, were sending me a round-trip bus ticket to come out to Colorado in early June. They were caretakers of the property of an old friend of theirs who had passed away in January, so a house was vacant in which I could stay during my visit. Ann's trailer house was too small, but I would eat my meals and spend my time with them. They promised to take me up into the mountains and see the things worth seeing in their area of beautiful western Colorado.

I was so excited. At last my dream of seeing Colorado and

the Rocky Mountains of John Denver was going to come true!

When people in my apartment building found out I was planning a bus trip to Colorado, some of them tried to talk me out of it.

"You're going to a high elevation," my neighbor Alice told me. "Don't you know that when you go to a place that high, there's not much oxygen? How are you going to be able to breathe?"

I wondered if there was too little air to breathe. Why did John Denver's album covers show forests with trees? I went to the library and researched Colorado thoroughly. I read everything I could get my hands on about its geology and the climate and elevation. I read all about high altitude pulmonary edema, and I grew scared. I was afraid I would be affected by the change in elevation, the diminished oxygen, and that I would be miserable the whole time.

When I talked to Ann, she reassured me that their home was only at 6,000 feet. There was nothing to worry about, she said. But I worried about going over the mountains, crossing the Eisenhower Tunnel and Vail Pass, which I found out were above 10,000 feet. What would happen to me then?

But the trip was almost cancelled. Two weeks before the trip, Kitty Girl got really sick. She had a urinary tract infection and I was afraid I was going to lose her. I called Ann to call off the trip, but she encouraged me to wait and see what the outcome would be. Sure enough, Kitty Girl recovered, but I had to find somebody who could come in and take care of my cats, who was willing to give Kitty Girl her medicine while I was gone.

I succeeded at finding someone, and on June 2, I took a taxi cab to the Greyhound bus station and embarked on a journey that would ultimately change my life.

STRANDED ON EARTH

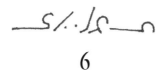

6

Rocky Mountain High

I was so excited, I couldn't sleep. It was practically impossible to sleep on that bus anyhow, since it was crowded and noisy. Traveling on the bus for two days, I wondered what Colorado would be like when I got there. I had a hard time sleeping. I was so excited. I had never met the people I was going to see. I remember being disappointed meeting other people in the past who turned out not to be what I expected them to be.

I pictured Ann's place to be high up in the mountains, with aspen trees and evergreen forests, and cool like the Swiss Alps with a beautiful landscape. I pictured Colorado to resemble the jackets of all the John Denver albums I owned.

But when I got to Colorado, it was grassy and flat for hours on the Eastern Slope. We traveled westward until we came to Denver and I could finally see the backdrop of the Rocky Mountains, though foggy through the city's population. I was not disappointed. I loved seeing the prairies, and got to see my first prairie dog town. Then we were in the mountains. Oh, they were splendid! So gigantic were those formations of rock and their snow-capped peaks, with evergreens and aspens and the bluest sky I'd ever seen.

The Colorado sky was such a deep blue, much much bluer than the sky in the East. And there was snow at the tops of the passes we went over. I already noticed that the air was fresher and cleaner than it was where I came from.

The terrain on the Western Slope of Colorado includes mesas and high deserts, in a semi-arid climate with real cactus. This made me think of all those westerns I like to watch on TV, and it also reminded me of my home world in Reticuli, with similar deserts. I wondered how many westerns had been filmed in Colorado.

It was Saturday, June 3, in the afternoon when I arrived at the Glenwood Springs bus terminal, weak and tired after my long ride. I suffer from a mild case of *Lupus*, which manifests a nasty case of arthritis. Strangely enough, my arthritis had not been bothering me for the last day or so.

It was such a beautiful, sunny, blue-skied day, and I was overjoyed when I saw the mountains for the first time. A few tears spilled and I had such a strong connection, for some reason.

Ann and Starhawk were there to greet me as I got off the bus. They seemed very happy to see me and were not shy about giving me a hug. They had brought with them their five-month-old puppy, Ranger, who was a black-and-white bundle of fur and energy. I later bonded with Ranger and love him. We went to a restaurant for a quick bite to eat, and then began the two-hour drive to their home.

We drove through a beautiful canyon. Early June is beautiful in Colorado. I loved the desert scenery mixed in with the mountain beauty. We stopped midway at a waterfall along the Crystal River, and when we got to Ann and Starhawk's place on the mesa, I breathed in the fresh air and felt good. The air was filled with sage smell. I had never smelled sage before except in a New Age book store. The view of the mountains was awesome.

I was tired when we finally arrived on Ann and Starhawk's mesa. The lack of sleep was beginning to catch up with me. The first thing I did was take a shower, and then they showed me where I would be staying, in the estate house that was vacant. Ann and Starhawk's home was a single-wide mobile home on the property, and they were planning to fix up and remodel the big house before moving into it. Their elderly friend had made his transition early in the year, and they were in the process of purchasing the property.

They wanted to be sure I would be okay staying there by myself. This was going to be fun. I had John Denver music and all sorts of New Age tapes to listen to, and I could burn my incense and draw. I had also brought along my bead work.

I couldn't wait to show Ann the present I had made her, so I got it out right away and was she ever surprised — I had made a pair of E.T. dolls for her, a set of twins — boy and girl — and she thought they were astounding. She displayed them proudly for anyone to see and thanked me profusely.

Because Ann had a job and had to go to work, Starhawk spent a lot of time with me. He was retired and stayed at home most of the time. Even though he struck me as being a very private man, Starhawk turned out to be a good listener. He was easy to talk to and I ended up baring my soul to him during my stay on the mesa. He asked me lots of questions, and I told him all about my past and the awful things people had done to me — especially Mr. Riley. Quite often it would make me cry. I felt like I was unloading all my pain and emotional turmoil. It was like I needed to get cleaned out, once and for all.

The three of us took trips around the area. We drove up into the mountains and I found that the higher altitude actually made me feel better. For weeks I had been worried about getting high altitude sickness. But the healthy air was healing and nurturing to me.

The view from the house was awesome. I would spend hours sitting at the big picture windows, looking out over the town and at the surrounding mountains, with the expensive binoculars they let me use. I couldn't get enough of those mountains. One night I looked out and saw a large amethyst-colored sphere near the large juniper tree in the front yard.

All the time I was in that house, I felt the elderly man's presence. Julian, they said his name was. I even saw his apparition a couple of times. I spent most my time with Ann and Starhawk over at their trailer, where we shared meals and many conversations.

In the evenings we would sit over on their deck and talk about space. I marveled at the sky. The stars seemed a lot closer and brighter, and every star was like a bright jewel. The Milky Way stretched from one end to the other overhead, like a shimmering curtain.

One night on their deck, I saw a meteor and several of my father's space craft. I knew I wasn't alone, and I took the meteor as a sign that a change was soon to occur. At the time I didn't realize how much change was going to happen, and how it was going to affect the rest of my life.

I gave Ann information about my home world and more about what I recalled of my crash in Roswell. She would ask questions and was always amazed at my responses.

While I was over at Ann and Starhawk's one evening during my visit, I received a clear message from the mountain known as Lamborn. It spoke to me. It said, "Welcome home, child. You have been away a very long time. Now you have come back to us."

The revelation hit me. I had been one of them — I had been a mountain long, long ago, long before humans had occupied that valley. And Mount Lamborn was my "mountain father." The mountain beside him, called Land's End, was my big brother, and the largest — the one tucked away in the West Elk Wilderness, was myself. I had once been Mount Gunnison.

When I told Ann and Starhawk that I was once a mountain, I think they thought I was joking. They didn't really say anything, but I could tell it was an idea that was difficult for them to grasp. But to me it was clear. I knew. That had been my connection.

On the weekend before I was to leave, they took me to Kebler Pass so we could have a picnic. The wildflowers were out and it was gorgeous. We were driving toward a mountain that had a steep face and I started to get an overwhelming feeling. Ann pointed out that we were approaching Mount Marcellina.

"Mother!" I cried out. Tears welled up. "Mother's, it's you! I'm your daughter! I've missed you, Mother ... Mother Marcellina..."

I don't know what Ann or Starhawk thought, but I felt a deep connection to that special mountain, Mount Marcellina. And that is how I came up with the name Marcellina for myself. From that day on I wanted to be called Marcellina Beckwith. The Beckwiths are a nearby pair of mountains that I knew to be my brothers.

On my second to the last evening in Colorado, there was a small gathering of like-minded people whom Ann had invited over to meet me. We met in the living room of the big house. Everyone was friendly and excited to meet me. Ann had told them a little about me, and most were probably curious, wondering what it would be like to meet an E.T. Everyone who gathered that June evening agreed that everything should be done to assist me in returning to this area, for good.

Jack, a man who had driven thirty miles to the meeting with his wife, even offered to drive me from my place back East, pulling his flatbed trailer. Starhawk said he would be willing to go, too, to help me make the move. I couldn't believe how generous and willing to help this loving group of people were. But first I had to find out if I could transfer my SSI and housing assistance, and then there was the problem of finding an affordable place to rent.

During the meeting I was asked to channel, once they found out that I could do that. Bashar came through me that evening, and the people gathered asked questions to which Bashar gave answers. Later on, Ann mentioned that she'd like to see if I could contact Julian, whose house we were in. He had made his transition in January, and everyone there had known and loved this man, who had died from complications following a bout with pneumonia.

I admitted that I had both felt and seen his presence in the house during my stay. I had seen a confused elderly man who appeared to be bothered by my presence in the house. He didn't seem to want to let go. Ann had the box containing his ashes still in the house, and they were wondering what would be the best thing to do with them. Should they scatter the ashes, or bury them somewhere on the property?

The next thing I knew, they turned out all the lights and lit a candle, then everyone joined hands in a circle and went into meditation. Dan (not his real name) led us, and after only a minute or so, I saw Julian, and immediately I fell into a trance. I don't remember anything that was said while I was in the trance state.

According to Ann and the others, I told them that their dear departed friend was afraid to go to the Light,but it was within reach. He seemed bewildered that he no longer had a body. They said I began communicating for this man in spirit, only I don't remember a thing that was said by him. Ann said he was concerned about all his things, particularly the house and his cars, so they spoke to him and reassured him that they were taking care of things and he had nothing more to worry about. Ann told him that even though they planned to change things in the house before they occupied it, it was to become a house of love and his things would go to people who would appreciate them.

Everyone then spoke gently to Julian, coaxing him with loving encouragement toward the Light. I apparently spoke for him and said he could see many people waiting for him as he slowly approached the Light. Ann told him that her father was there, holding out his hand, and then Julian crossed into the Light and was free. Others could see him soaring like an eagle.

I awoke at that point and saw that everyone's faces were full of joy and relief. There was such a light feeling in the room as we slowly brought the lights back on. I was extremely tired, the way I've always gotten when I've been in a trance. But from that time on, I no longer felt the haunting presence in the big house.

It was eleven o'clock at night when everybody left. It had been a tremendous meeting and I received so many hugs. Even though Dan and his wife had said they had to leave early because of an early morning commitment, they ended up staying the entire time. Dan's wife, Cassie (not her real name), hugged me for a long time and told me how glad she had been to meet me. She looked forward to seeing a lot more of me. I had so many new friends all of a sudden.

On Wednesday I had to leave and go back home. I was not looking forward to it. But I was encouraged by all the wonderful new friends and I began to look forward to a day real soon when I would be returning to my beloved mountains. During the long and tiresome bus ride home, I reflected on my eleven-day visit, all the beautiful things I had seen, all the friendly people, and I wished with all my heart I would be able to return to Colorado soon. Riding through Kansas on my way home, I saw a pretty rainbow against a purplish maroon sky.

Khinyeo told me, "You must relocate. If you stay in the East, you will die within five years." That scared me.

My friends back in the city were alarmed when I told them I was planning to move to Colorado. They didn't believe it would really happen. Of course, I realized it might take some time. I didn't expect anything to come of it until the autumn. Plus there was so much to consider. So many plans and preparations.

Then, one night, about a week after I returned from Colorado, I got a call from Ann and Starhawk. Starhawk had found a house for me. It was a little blue cozy house in town that had a bedroom and an extra large back room that had been converted from a garage. It was available immediately and Starhawk had put down the security deposit on it. He wondered if I could be ready to move within another week. He and Jack were making plans to drive out and get me.

I couldn't believe it. It was happening. I was moving to Colorado!

_S/. Jℓ_

7

A New Life

On the 29th of June 2000, shortly before the anniversary of my crash at Roswell, I arrived at my new home in the mountains, after a long ride in Jack's Suburban, accompanied by Starhawk and my two cats, who were in a cage on the trailer. As I had left the apartment complex, everyone stood outside and waved goodbye to me. We had driven practically non-stop after packing up all my things over the course of two days. It had taken us another two days on the road. I know we had unseen help from above on our journey.

The following is the write-up Ann put into the August *Star Beacon* about my move.

SANNI ARRIVES IN (COLORADO)

We call it a miracle. Everything happened so fast, it has left us amazed. As you read in the July *Star Beacon*, in early June, Sanni came to western Colorado for a visit, hoping beyond hope there would be some way she could leave her depressing situation in (the East) and make a new life for herself in Colorado.

The word was sent out. The call for help rang out among *Star Beacon* readers, and now, less than two months later, Sanni is living in Colorado. She has left her life in (the East) behind, and with the help of her new friends and many generous *Star Beacon* readers, Sanni's dream is coming true. She is surrounded by her beloved mountains and is finding the means to heal her mind, her body and her spirit.

First, I want to thank all of you readers who sent in donations for Sanni and encouraged her. She is extremely grateful and overwhelmed by the love and support she has received in such a short time. Just let me explain what happened when a few people committed themselves to a mission of helping a fellow light worker in need.

It hadn't been two weeks since Sanni left on the bus, crying for fear she'd never be back, that (Starhawk) found a suitable rental in our small town... Within days, Jack and (Starhawk) were prepared to drive Jack's Suburban, pulling a flatbed trailer, to (Sanni's state). Jack's wife had just had surgery on her shoulder, and (Starhawk) and I were in the process of moving. It was not the best time to drop everything and drive across country to bring Sanni to Colorado. But Spirit was in charge.

The men drove straight to (Sanni's state) without stopping, in just 31 hours. One drove while the other slept. It took two days to pack and load up Sanni's belongings. Then they began the long trek west.

Jack says the "synchronicity of it" convinced him that this mission of getting Sanni to Colorado was of utmost importance. Both he and (Starhawk) felt strongly compelled to act on her behalf, despite the circumstances in their lives.

Coming into Topeka, Kansas, the trailer blew a tire. Jack pulled the vehicle off the interstate and within five minutes a state patrol car stopped to help. (Starhawk) was in the process of changing the tire, but the patrolman cautioned him not to. The patrolman immediately went to work changing the tire himself! Now how often does it happen that you break down on the interstate and there is a state patrol car right there? And how many policemen have ever offered to change the tire for you? Somebody was watching out for these people!

After the tire was changed, they drove into Topeka to locate a replacement tire. The tire shop was busy and somehow Jack got sold the wrong kind of tire. They had just started out on I-70 when the new tire blew! And again, a state patrolman was right there within five minutes to help them out! This time, when they went back to the tire shop, they talked to the business owner, who remedied his mistake and gave them the proper tires.

On June 29, after 44 hours on the road, three tired light workers arrived with two stressed-out cats. The trip had taken its toll on Jack and (Starhawk), who were worn out. Sanni was worried about her cats, who had never traveled such a long journey before. But they got her into her house that evening and began unloading her things. She was home at last!

The next couple of weeks, while I was vacationing in Wisconsin, (Starhawk) helped Sanni visit the Social Security office and all the places she had to go to get her affairs in order. It was not an easy task, but thank goodness (he) was willing to step in and be her "guardian."

Sanni reminds me that I forgot to mention one important thing in the July article that happened when she was visiting. One day we drove out to Needle Rock, near Crawford, so that Sanni could experience the energy vortex there. She had been telling me how very much she wanted to see an eagle while she was in Colorado. It was the thing she wanted to see most. Of course, we couldn't promise her an eagle. The best time for seeing them is December and January, near rivers. But on the way out the back road, suddenly a large golden eagle swooped down in front of the car, carrying a prairie dog it had just picked up in a field. I stopped the car and the golden eagle brushed right past the passenger window, where Sanni was sitting. Then we watched the regal bird take off in flight. Sanni was elated.

I want to mention here that during our journey out West I felt there was a white light bubble around Jack's vehicle and that Yahweh was watching over us.

During the two weeks in July that Ann and her son were gone, visiting their relatives in the Midwest, Starhawk helped me get settled and drove me to the county and state offices I needed to visit to be sure my affairs were in order because of the move. I don't know what I would have done without Starhawk during that time. He really bent over backwards to help me.

Also, when I first arrived in Colorado I had a lot of difficulty walking. But it wasn't long before that changed. Eventually I was able to take hikes up in the mountains with some of my new friends, and even climbed Mount Lamborn.

The Second Annual Love and Light Conference was held in August. Ann and Starhawk were in charge of the light workers' conference that brought in speakers and workshops about a variety of topics, including UFOs, healing, channeling and more. Even though I didn't like being around large groups of people, I attended part of the conference and met some people who would become important in my life.

One of these was John Robert Feather, a healer from Virginia, who was very kind and generous. He talked about Perfect Health Vibrations and performed healings on people for free. He had a wonderful energy to be around. I met Cindy and Daniel Nichols from Canon City, who told me they wanted me to come stay with them for a few days and see that part of Colorado. And then there was Lilian from Washington state, who wanted to interview me for one of her cable TV programs, "Persons of High Strangeness." She invited me to come to Washington and stay with her. With Lilian was Monica Smith, and we connected right away. When Monica found out that I had an affinity for mountains, she began speaking in "mountain" and I understood her! We talked to each other, rock to rock — and it must have been quite a sight for others.

On Sunday, the last day of the conference, I just happened to be in the room when the Lakota spiritual leader, Standing Elk, walked in. Standing Elk had driven all the way from South Dakota just to speak at Ann's Love and Light Conference. He is a famous leader among Native Americans and has put on numerous Star Knowledge Conferences around the country since the 1990s. I went over to Standing Elk and told him who I was and that my grandmother had been a Native American. For some reason I couldn't stop talking. He listened as I told him about my crash at Roswell and the symbols I drew.

This caught Standing Elk's attention. I found out later that he had received symbols from space beings and had been interpreting them as well as presenting the information in his talks about universal symbols and their meanings. During his afternoon talk at the conference, he brought up the fact that he had met me and that the subject of the symbols had come up.

It was that night, after the conference was over, that a few select people went over to Ann and Starhawk's house. They were now living in the big estate house, where I had stayed while visiting them. Standing Elk was holding ceremony in their living room, and he had asked that I be present, so Starhawk had driven over to get me and bring me up on the mesa. Cindy and Daniel were there, and so were some others from the conference.

The ceremony was awesome. Standing Elk invited me to

channel, if I felt the urge, and I definitely did feel the urge. For hours we sat there and sang, chanted and drummed. I spoke in my Native language, and some in Pleiadian, and then in Lakota. The ceremony was videotaped by Standing Elk, and Ann has it recorded on an audio tape. Standing Elk said it was important to document me and that transcripts would be available of what we were accomplishing that night. The whole evening was an unforgettable experience, and the energy that was felt on the mesa that night was unlike anything I had ever felt before.

Ann mentioned that on Monday morning she had to get up early to go to work. When she stepped outside first thing, she clearly heard Standing Elk's voice singing in his Native tongue and it echoed through the valley below their mesa.

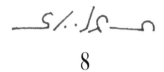

8

Leaving the Old Behind

My first fall season in Colorado meant having a yard to rake and take care of. I met a lot of new people and celebrated my first real birthday party in early September. Ann and Starhawk invited all their friends from the group that had met in June, and there was cake and ice cream, candles to blow out, and presents — I was thrilled. I had never celebrated birthdays back where I used to live, because no one seemed to care.

Starhawk had found a used three-wheel bike for me to ride downtown that had a basket. Otherwise I had to walk ten blocks to the center of town for groceries or to visit the library. I soon mastered the bike and gave it a name: Wind Horse.

I made friends with the ladies who worked at the library. They helped me in so many ways, even giving me rides now and then. I began to spend more and more time on the public computers at the library, looking things up on the Internet, and using the e-mail address Ann had helped me obtain.

My older cat, Kitty Girl, fell ill once more. This time she was hemorrhaging, and I knew it was her time to leave. It was a very sad day when Starhawk helped me take Kitty Girl to the local veterinarian to be put to sleep. We buried my beautiful cat up on the mesa, in the woods.

Shortly after that someone gave me a black kitten. I named him Lamborn after one of the nearby mountain peaks. Lamborn eventually became a good companion to my other cat, E.T.

My friend Cassie from the group that had helped bring me to Colorado came over every Wednesday evening to visit. Her daughter was attending a class in town and she had time to kill, so we made a habit out of it. Cassie was very nice and her friendship meant a lot to me.

Sometimes Jack would make the trip over to see me and take me out for a hamburger and a drive. He was especially interested in my channeling Bashar, which I did often for him. Then he introduced me to a couple from a nearby town who were also interested in hearing what Bashar had to say. We soon had regular meetings in which I would channel Bashar.

For Christmas that first year, these friends invited everyone in the group over and they presented me with my Christmas present: an electronic keyboard. I loved it and was able to channel Home World music on it. I felt so blest having all these new light worker friends.

Both Thanksgiving and Christmas Day were spent up on the mesa with Ann and Starhawk. They had a house full of guests, including two of Ann's sons and the daughter of the elderly friend, Julian, who had died, who came to visit her old home a final time. Mary had Downs Syndrome and was living in California. Even though she wasn't interested in space or UFOs, we got along fine.

It was wonderful to have an adopted family to spend holidays with after so many years of being alone. It used to be Christmas was just another day in my monotonous routine of living. But Ann and Starhawk made me part of their family, and for that I will always be grateful.

On Monday evening, Jan. 8, 2001, Standing Elk, the Lakota spiritual leader from the Yankton Sioux Tribe in South Dakota, wanted to hold Ceremony to celebrate the Lunar Eclipse. He and a small group of friends from Fort

Collins and South Dakota came to the valley, to Ann and Starhawk's mesa, and invited anyone who wanted to come to be included. One of the Native singers was Standing Elk's grandson.

After a delicious meal of bear stew, provided by Ann and Starhawk's neighbor, Peggy French, they set up for the ceremony and the guests began to arrive. I was among them. Since I had gone into ceremony with Standing Elk last August, on the final night of the Love and Light Conference, I had discovered that Standing Elk is my spiritual brother.

Quite unexpectedly, there came about a "naming ceremony" for me. I revealed to Standing Elk that my Cherokee grandmother (now in the world beyond) had given me my Native name: White Buffalo Medicine Calf Woman. Standing Elk proceeded with the naming ceremony with a local light worker woman standing in as my honorary "grandmother."

After the naming ceremony, we had the lunar eclipse ceremony in which the women in the group were asked to reveal any messages they received from Spirit. Standing Elk said that this lunar eclipse, being a Cancerian Moon, was to focus on "the home, nurturing and security."

The drumming and songs uplifted many of us that evening, along with the passing of the sacred pipe. Afterward, Standing Elk visited with me, and I felt honored.

I started working for Ann once a month, helping her process her newsletter for the mailing. She gave me the job of collating and folding the papers, sealing and stamping them. I still look forward to helping each month with *The Star Beacon*. I also began house-sitting for Ann and Starhawk when they would go away for a weekend. Their dog, Ranger, grew into a wonderful animal, and I even learned to take care of feeding and watering their mules and chickens. I always look forward to being asked to house sit on the mesa because it is so beautiful up there. I can pick all the sage I want, to make smudge sticks, and the dog and I take walks.

My house-sitting skills came to the attention of others around me. I was already good friends with my next-door neighbors, and when spring came around we visited quite often in the yard. The neighbor man offered to mow my lawn several times, and they noticed that I seemed to have a way with plants. They came to depend on me for watering the plants in their greenhouse and taking care of their lawn while they were gone on some trips that summer.

Then I met another neighbor, Peggy, who lived in the next block. It was her husband's three-wheel bike that Starhawk had bought for me. We got to be truly good friends, and Peggy and I would take evening walks together. Her husband, who was 90 years old, was not doing well health-wise. I was blessed with new friends as well as my old friends from back East.

A close friend I'd known in the East kept in touch with me after my move. I'll call her Nancy, but that isn't her real name. She began showing interest in moving to Colorado and we talked about her coming out and getting her own place nearby. Nancy was on some kind of assistance, but she worked a part-time job at night as a security guard. She wanted to relocate and be my companion. Since she drove and had her own car, she could take me places, which would be less of a burden on Ann and Starhawk.

The more we talked about it, the more realistic it became. Ann and Starhawk were all for it and encouraged Nancy to move to Colorado. By March of that first year it was all settled. Nancy had given notice at her job and was packing up her things. She purchased a one-way bus ticket for me to come out and the plan was for me to ride with her back to

Colorado.

As the time approached for me to return to my old home, I grew apprehensive and unsure whether this was what I wanted. I missed my old friends and was looking forward to visiting with them again. But for some reason I had a funny feeling about Nancy.

When I arrived at the bus depot around midnight, there was no one there to meet me as planned. Nancy had apparently gotten mixed up about my time of arrival, or she simply forgot. Anyway, I called her and she drove right down to get me.

Things did not start out on a good note. I was tired, cranky and upset at Nancy for not being at the bus station when I arrived. Plus I noticed she was one big bundle of nerves — different from the way I remembered her. She was exceptionally skinny, having lost quite a bit of weight.

There was nothing to eat at Nancy's apartment except some cold left-over oatmeal. She drank cup after cup of coffee and smoked cigarettes endlessly. Her hands shook and she was not friendly. She snapped at me over every little thing and put me down at every opportunity. I noticed in her bathroom she had burnt spoons and a rubber tourniquet, as well as some bags of white powder that looked like sugar. While I was there she accused me of trying to steal her spoons.

I called Ann and Starhawk the next day and cried into the telephone, explaining the situation I found myself in. Nancy took hold of the phone and explained to them what a mess I was, that all because she had forgotten when to pick me up at the bus station, things had fallen apart between us.

After a long time on the telephone, Ann and Starhawk convinced Nancy that things would settle down and we'd be all right once we got on the road. I wasn't so sure.

Over the next few days I did get to visit my old friends

and I even saw my old therapist. She was pleased that I seemed to be doing well in Colorado and told me how proud she was of me.

It was a day or two before Nancy and I were planning to pack all her boxes into her car and head out to Colorado. She had arranged for her mail to be forwarded to my address until she had her own place. Nancy was especially on edge that night. Her eyes were bloodshot, the apartment reeked of cigarette smoke, and she trembled more than usual.

What bothered me the most was the handgun she had laid beside her chair. We continued to argue and I was afraid that at any moment she would go berserk and point the gun right at me.

"You ought to be locked up, you know," Nancy told me with the cigarette dangling from her dry, cracked lips. "You're nuts. Everybody knows you are."

I began to cry again.

"If you give me any trouble... any trouble at all... I'm gonna make a phone call and they're gonna come and take you to a psycho ward."

I was terribly frightened by the look in her eyes. *She* was the one who needed to be in the psycho ward — not me! I didn't dare say a word, because that gun was loaded and I was afraid she'd use it. How could my old friend have changed into this monster? I suspected drugs to be the cause. She was a total mess!

I don't know how I did it, but finally I was able to convince Nancy that maybe I should take the bus back to Colorado and let her drive there by herself. She had barely enough money to buy another bus ticket for me. I ended up giving her all that I had — my food money — and I told her I would pay her back for both bus tickets.

We made another telephone call to Ann and Starhawk,

who were disappointed at how things had turned out for us. They agreed to meet me at the bus station when I got into Glenwood Springs.

I was so relieved to return to Colorado and my true friends and beloved mountains. The trip back East had traumatized me and I didn't care if Nancy showed up or not. I wasn't convinced we could ever still be friends.

As it turned out, Nancy and a friend of hers did drive out to Colorado. She left a message on Ann's answering machine from a motel in Carbondale. She must have been blinded by her own conception of Colorado, because the message said she was going back, that she had found it to be ugly, and someone had lied to her about the place. That was all she said. Apparently she had driven through the area on April Fool's Day, but hadn't bothered to call any of us or make an effort to find where I lived. How she could call our beautiful town "ugly" simply does not make sense.

All I can say is I've never heard from Nancy since. Her mail kept coming to my address and eventually I had to contact the post office to get them to stop delivering it to me. I kept an envelope with cash in it to give Nancy for buying the bus tickets, but she never contacted me or Ann or Starhawk. Her whereabouts remain a mystery to this day.

_S/..J—_

9

Return to Roswell

It was July and Ann held the Third Annual Love and Light Conference, which I attended. She agreed to display my E.T. dolls at the conference, but somebody complained about them, because they were Grays, and so Ann decided to take them down. She was upset that people found them offensive, and I was devastated to think that anyone would suggest that I was from the dark side.

I had discovered, over my e-mail contact on the Internet at the library, that some people considered the Gray race to be evil. That is not so. Apparently these people are mixed up with the Reptoid race. Zeta Reticulans are Insectoid, not of the reptilian origin — and there is a big difference.

At the time the conference was going on, I met Carol Syska from Roswell, New Mexico, who had heard about me and was traveling through with an RV with her sister. They stopped at my place and we had a brief visit, but we connected and she invited me down to Roswell sometime in the future. I was excited to have met Carol, who had worked at the UFO museum there in Roswell.

About that same time, my dear friend Cassie dropped a bomb on me. She told me she was no longer going to come over on Wednesday nights, that she had been given the message to ease up on our friendship, due to being overwhelmed.

I did not understand what she meant. Overwhelmed? By what? She simply said she was experiencing too much of the

"Gray" energy and had to stop seeing me for a while.

Well, I was deeply hurt. I could not understand why she would cut our friendship off just like that. I thought she was my friend, and here she was telling me she couldn't be my friend any more. I guess I'll never understand humans.

Other people in the group that had helped bring me to Colorado also seemed to be having second thoughts about me. For one thing, Jack's wife had been upset that he had taken off with Starhawk to bring me to Colorado, because she was having surgery right then. She has resented me ever since, and has now forbidden her husband from contacting me. This hurt deeply, for I never meant to cause her or anybody any pain.

Another woman from the group who had been so kind to me also turned her back on me, claiming that I was not "of the Light." Only Ann and Starhawk seemed to not let other people's opinions and judgments affect them where I was concerned.

In November 2001 my friend Lilian from Washington state invited me to come visit and stay for three weeks. She wanted me to appear as a special guest on her TV show, "A Person of High Strangeness," which aired on local cable channels. I took the bus to Washington during that cold and gloomy time of the year. I stayed part of the time with Lilian and part of the time with a couple of her friends.

The television show went well and I demonstrated trance channeling on that program. Again, I made many new friends and got to visit the ocean as well as Mount Rainier. Lilian is a most interesting individual, having been born in Algeria and then sold as a slave by her grandmother. She was raised in Germany by adopted parents, and then spent some of her early adulthood in Canada. Like me, she considers herself a hybrid, since her biological father was allegedly a "space man" her mother met on the Algerian plains. That seemed to be the likely reason why her skin was white when she was born of the black race. If you are interested in reading about Lilian's unusual and fascinating autobiography, go to her Web site at www.Psygeria.com and order *And The Moral of the Story Is... One Person at a Time.*

I was home for the holiday season. Ann and Starhawk had me up on their mesa for Christmas again that year. After all the gifts had been opened, they said to wait, that there was one more present to open. Ann and her sons left the room and when they came back in, there was a huge cardboard box all gift-wrapped with a bow. I couldn't believe it was for me.

When I opened that box, I was flabbergasted! It was a computer — my very own personal computer! I had never in my life received a more wonderful present than that computer. They explained it was a used one, and they had found somebody who wanted to donate the computer to me. Ann's son had set everything up for me — even the e-mail program. I couldn't wait to get it home and get everything hooked up. For the first month I had free Internet service for obtaining my e-mail, and then I had to go with Ann to the local telephone company and set up my own account.

The computer changed my life. Even though it was not the best computer on the market, and it was slow, I loved it. I quickly learned how to get around on it, and how to set up different backgrounds on the desktop and play games. I no longer had to rely on the library's computers, but I decided I would still go there once a week or so, to stay in touch with my librarian friends.

E-mail opened up a whole new world for me. I soon had friends all over the country and around the world. People wanted to know more about me, and most of them accepted who I was and were eager to read the information I had to share. I became assistant manager of a Web site about space and moderator for some chat rooms. I spent hours on that computer, often staying up very late at night.

I had kept in touch with Carol Syska from Roswell, New Mexico, and we talked about my making a bus trip to Roswell later that year. She thought it would be better for me to come when it wasn't so terribly hot. I began to save money for that important trip.

There was no Love and Light conference in 2002. Ann had planned one, but because of a number of circumstances she had to call it off. Summer passed and with autumn in full swing I arranged with Carol to go to Roswell for a week.

It was October and Red Mountain Pass was gorgeous as the bus drove across it toward Durango. We stopped in Silverton for a restaurant break and I loved that mountain town. I arrived in Albuquerque later that day, where Carol and her sister met me, then drove me the remaining hours to Roswell.

Needless to say, I was excited. Khinyeo had told me time and again that I needed to go back to my crash site and face the shame of what I had done, and to ask forgiveness from the Council. This quest needed to be completed before I could be allowed to go "Home."

The following excerpt is from the article Carol Syska wrote for the November 2002 *Star Beacon.*

Sanni's return to Roswell, New Mexico

As part of Sanni's mission here on Earth, she was to return to the site of her crash in 1947. On Sunday, Oct. 6, Sanni took a bus to Albuquerque, where she was met by her hostess from Roswell, Carol Syska, and Carol's sister, Pauline Whisenhunt.

On the four-hour drive to Roswell from Albuquerque, Sanni was exposed to the high desert country with mountains in the distance — one of those being the one called Capitan — the site of Sanni's crash in 1947.

Monday morning found the three of them visiting with Florence Alexander, who completed the threesome that had first met Sanni in July 2001 during a stop in (western) Colorado. Monday afternoon they went to the International UFO Museum and Research Center, where Sanni was introduced to the story of the Roswell Incident as was published in various newspapers across the United States in 1947.

Sanni was very interested in the MJ-12 material and other information regarding cover-ups by the government. Pictures of sightings over the years, accounts by eyewitnesses and photos of crop circles she found extremely interesting. Sanni gave Carol lots of new information about some of the subjects, such as various crafts, what they were used for, their propulsion systems, their protective systems, and other kinds of aliens besides the Grays, and where they were from in the galaxies.

Sanni was very interested in the alien dummy that was featured in the movie *Roswell*. She very quickly pointed out some errors, but agreed the likeness was an excellent symbol to help get the truth of the matter out to the public.

Tuesday was very cloudy and there was a slight mist falling when Sanni and Carol were picked up by Dave and Nettie Crocker for a trip to the crash site. This particular site has been referred to for several years as the "Ragsdale Site," because it was first made public by a man named Jim Ragsdale, who was an eyewitness to the 1947 crash. The site is located approximately sixty miles from Roswell and can only be reached with a four-wheel drive vehicle, unless one chooses to hike a couple of miles through very rough terrain. Dave drove his truck all the way. Just as we arrived, it started raining and we had a good shower before it stopped. The rest of the day was perfect with the sun actually coming out before it was over.

Sanni's return to the site of her crash was very emotional, but after several minutes of communication on her part, while she was very close to the large rock against which her craft had come to rest, she was able to reconnect with her crew members and her Council.

After her connection and communication was over, she told us she felt as though a heavy load had lifted off her shoulders. She reported that the Council had said she was forgiven and could now return home one of these days. Then, she roamed all over the area and, via flashbacks, recalled many of her experiences.

Wednesday was another day spent in the Roswell area. Since Sanni's favorite singer is John Denver, we showed her the area of town and the block where John lived as a boy. Homes on the block have been torn down and the post office and bank fill the area now. Then we moved on to the area where the hospital was in which John Denver was born. That, too, has disappeared, and in its place are the new city office buildings, where the city government is housed. John's father was in the military, stationed at Walker Air Base, when his famous-to-be son was born.

The next stop on our tour was to the airport area, where the famous "Hangar 84" is located. A private company now uses the facility and, of course, it is fenced in completely. However, we could see through the fence. Immediately Sanni started having flashbacks, which she described vividly — how material was separated into different piles, how many of the workers were without shirts because the weather there was so hot, and how she and the other aliens were put into wooden crates with cedar chips thrown around and these crates were nailed shut and hauled off by some kind of vehicle to the "big birds," and then flown East.

As we were leaving the area, we noticed a fenced-in location that was pretty well filled with weeds but had some items protruding through. I thought they were just scrap pieces of old aircraft, but Sanni knew otherwise and so we took a closer look. There were four models of different spacecraft in the yard. Sanni proceeded to describe each one and how big the actual craft would be, how it would operate, and for what purpose.

Later, I remembered that at one time, a year or so ago, a couple of these models had been on display at the Mall north of Roswell. When observing them at that time, I just thought they were someone's idea of what spacecraft could possibly look like, and they were not taken seriously by anyone.

In summary, I would like to say that when I first heard of Sanni and even after talking to her a few times, I was very skeptical of the entire story. But over the past year and a half of communication with her, I have swayed heavily in her favor. Now, after her visit to Roswell and hearing her story over and over — and the many different aspects of it — I have to say that I now believe her 100 percent. Her reactions at the crash site, at the museum, and at Hangar 84 were such that I don't believe anyone witnessing them could think otherwise. Her immediate replies to any and all questions asked of her were of such nature that I don't believe anyone could have all that knowledge so readily available without having to think about it before speaking. I have heard many speakers on the Roswell topic and they all hesitate from time to time before speaking — but not Sanni.

She is truly a highly intelligent being, and I feel very honored to have made her acquaintance and gained her friendship. She should be highly respected by all and we should listen to her with our minds wide open. We may not have believed such as this in the past, and it does seem farfetched even now, but I can remember when going to the moon was an impossibility, much less thinking of going into outer space!

By the way, they (the aliens) do believe in a Supreme Being who created us *all*, not just the earth and its solar system! Thank you, Sanni, for sharing some of your knowledge with me.

When I went to the site of my accident, I saw four balls of light that were meant for me to see. These four balls came together as one ball and entered into me. The Council said it was the energy of the four crew members who perished that night.

While at the crash site, I recognized the terrain, the landscape around me, as it being the site of where my accident occurred. I also had intense flashbacks to that night in 1947. I had felt a strong surge of energy through me while there.

Also, since my return to Colorado, there was a strong pull to return to Roswell — maybe in a year or so — and possibly relocate there.

While at the museum, I was overwhelmed by my memories flooding back to me. Later that week we visited the Pecos Desert and I was impressed with the energies there plus the wonderful cactus, plants and crystals.

My Council watched me the whole time that I was there. While going through Aztec, New Mexico, on the bus, my implant started humming so loud, it blocked the sounds of the bus and the people talking. Every time I closed my eyes, I saw a crash occurring. There had been a large ship that had gone down in Aztec in 1948. It was 90 feet in diameter. My implant hummed till I arrived in Roswell, then it stopped.

Sometime after I returned from Roswell, I began receiving e-mails, then telephone calls, from a professor whom I had not met, but whom Carol had talked to about me. I will call him Professor Sims, although that is not his real name. The professor was extremely interested in me and what I had to share, having been convinced by Carol that I was genuine and had my memories from the 1947 crash as well as a wealth of information about space and E.T.s in general.

Since the professor was writing a book about extraterrestrials, he wanted to tap the information and use it in his book. I was agreeable as long as Khinyeo did not object to what I shared with Earth humans. And so began a long and intense communication, often on a daily basis, with this Professor Sims, who was grateful for all information I could give him. And I gave him a lot!

The months passed and the professor wanted me to return to Roswell for a visit and to meet him. I would be staying with him at his house, and he would introduce me to his fiancee. It was arranged for me to go in March. Again I took the Greyhound bus to Albuquerque, and this time Professor Sims and his fiancee met me and drove me to Roswell.

For the most part, I had a wonderful time. They treated me like their long lost, beloved daughter, and I got to see Carol again. But Professor Sims made me work hard at his information-gathering sessions. He wanted me to channel information as well, and that always leaves me exhausted. I ended up more than ready to go home at the end of a week.

Before I left, the professor took me to a local computer

store and had me pick out a new computer — complete with all the bells and whistles — and he wanted it to be a state-of-the-art computer so that I would be able to work on it without getting bogged down. We chose a Pentium IV that reminded me of a space ship because the CPU tower had all kinds of colored lights that blinked on and off. The computer had a cordless mouse and keyboard, and the professor insisted on including a color printer along with it.

I was thrilled! The professor paid for the new computer and the shop said it would be delivered to me via UPS the following week. This was to be my payment for helping Professor Sims with his upcoming book.

When I got back home to Colorado, I was tired but happy. The professor had also arranged for me to attend the Sacred Hoop Festival in Silver City, New Mexico, in June. I had already met a woman who was connected to that event, and we had taken to each other right away. And so I was looking forward to returning to New Mexico, this time up in the mountains.

The new computer arrived and I was so excited, I assembled it myself and had it up and working before Ann's son could come over. It was wonderful having a fast computer, but I did not like the cordless mouse. It required a frequent change of batteries, which soon became an expense. Eventually the keyboard quit working, and I had to go out and purchase a new keyboard — this time with a cord. At the same time I got myself a mouse with a cord.

By the time summer arrived, the professor and my friendship began to deteriorate. He had become more demanding in his requests for information. I was grateful for the computer and all he had done for me, but I felt pressured and I didn't like that feeling. Khinyeo warned me to be careful. Professor Sims suddenly put a list of demands before me. He insisted, for one thing, that I give up some of my old habits in order to be a "pure channel." He wanted me to quit cigarettes. I was reluctant to do this, because I had tried quitting before, when I first came to Colorado, and it was extremely difficult. I discovered later that the occasional American Spirit cigarette grounded me and kept me from being too stressed out.

Since I wouldn't do everything he said, the professor grew increasingly annoyed with me and criticized everything I did or said. This created tension between us that eventually led to our parting of ways. I finally had to tell Professor Sims that my Council instructed me not to have anything more to do with him.

STRANDED ON EARTH

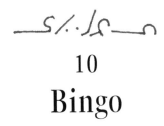

10

Bingo

In June 2003 I returned to New Mexico, this time to Silver City, to take part in the Sacred Hoop Fest. While at the Sacred Hoop gathering, I helped call in ships. Some were seen overhead by those of us in that ceremony. I received messages in Pleiadian and Zeti which I translated to the group.

Grandmother Louise told me that she saw my father, Khinyeo, inside her tent one night.

While at the gathering, I was awakened by a light inside my tent and I saw Khinyeo kneeling over me. The next day a friend that was in a tent nearby said she woke up and saw that my tent was surrounded by objects moving around it and a large disk-like object was at tree-top level near my tent.

I met Mr. Timm at the Sacred Hoop Fest. Roy Timm is a senior Star Person who lives in Pendleton, Oregon. He has written a book, *Northwest History of Saucers, ETs, Abductions and More*, and has researched UFOs for more than fifty years. When I first saw Mr. Timm sitting there, I recognized him and went up and introduced myself.

We had made a flyover of his ranch in Oregon prior to the crash in 1947. And we took photos. We could age-progress or regress the photo to make the person look older or younger if we were to have contact with that person in another time. This technology was more advanced than your current photography.

I said to Mr. Timm, "I've been wanting to meet you for a

long, long time." And the first thing we did was hug one another. Then he started asking me questions about the pyramids and things like that, and I answered his questions.

Mr. Timm and I have remained good friends ever since we met in New Mexico. We have been on radio programs together, and he has helped me in many ways, including the submission of copyright papers so that my name can be included on the music CD I helped make in New Mexico with Maya Rose. Titled *We Are Here Again,* the CD includes singing, drumming and chanting in both Pleiadian and my Zeti tongue. Some people claimed there was a spaceship overhead while we were making the CD. When I stepped outside, I sensed the ship was cloaked.

In the summer of 2003 I made my acquaintance with Mr. Bingo, a full-blooded springer spaniel, whose owner was looking for a good home for him. Well, I already had my two cats: E.T., who came with me from the East, and Lamborn, whom I'd had since he was a kitten shortly after I moved to Colorado and lost Kitty Girl. I wasn't supposed to have pets in my rental, but the landlord graciously allowed my cats because I was taking such good care of his property.

I decided to ask if it was all right to have a dog as well. The property manager was reluctant, but I was allowed to keep Mr. Bingo, so I took him. He was a young dog and had not been fixed, so that was the first thing — to take him to the vet to get castrated.

Bingo was good company for me. We bonded and I loved him like a child. But he had never been trained, so when I would leave the house he would cry and whine the whole time I was gone. My neighbor called to complain about the noise he made. I soon felt as though I couldn't leave the house, because Bingo would put up such a fuss. I think he had an attachment disorder, where he couldn't stand to be alone.

No matter how hard I tried to discipline and train him, that dog never learned to stay by himself without crying and whining. Yet I still loved him so much.

I was house-sitting for Ann and Starhawk one weekend in the fall, and Mr. Bingo took after Ann's chickens while he was on a 40-foot-long chain. When I wasn't minding him, he managed to kill two of her hens.

I felt devastated. How could this happen? Ann would never forgive me! When they got home and saw what had happened, they were naturally upset, but not as sick as I was. And later, when Ann said that she couldn't have Bingo back up on the mesa, on account of the chickens, I didn't know what I was going to do. Would I never be allowed to house sit there again?

Bingo turned out to be a lot more work than I had anticipated. I was starting to feel guilty when I had to run an errand downtown. I bought a muzzle for him, but he hated it and sometimes managed to get it off. I lived in constant fear of my neighbor calling and complaining about Bingo's barking.

Finally, the day came when I decided Bingo had to go. Two friends from the Sacred Hoop Fest in New Mexico drove up to get me just before Christmas. They said Bingo could come along, so I arranged to have Ann look in on my cats while I was gone, and I went to New Mexico for the holidays.

The first thing Bingo did when we arrived at our destination was to chase after a herd of javalinas, those wild pigs that run around down there, and he went after my friends' cat. Things didn't go well on that trip.

There was an interesting event that occurred while I was there. When my friend and I were coming home from the grocery store, she grew excited about a light and pointed it out to me. It was a reddish purple light that was too low in the sky to be an airplane. It would blink on and off and then reappear in a different section of the sky. I knew from its actions that it wasn't an airplane, and this was near the airport.

The week after Christmas they drove me back to Colorado, and on the way we stopped at a rest area where there were lots of rock formations. It was full moon and we saw a blue shaft of light emerge from a mountain. They kept asking me what it was, and I said there was a portal there, and inside the mountain was a base. It was at that rest area that I found my Angel.

She ran across the road as our car pulled out. My friend got out of the car and walked over to the bushes and called the animal, which came right over. She brought it into the car. It was a full-grown, long-haired Himalayan cat that someone must have abandoned out there in the middle of nowhere. She was nothing but skin and bones. The first thing I did was give her some water. She tried to eat a cracked hard-boiled egg we had along, and I offered her some of Bingo's food. She was so weak, she hardly had any strength to eat.

She laid in my lap the rest of the way home. I ended up keeping her and nursed her back to health, where she spent most of her time on my water heater, where it was warm and cozy. I called her Angel Girl because I felt she was a gift to me from Yahweh. To see her now you wouldn't believe how emaciated she once was. She is a beautiful animal, very loving, and so heavy now, she's hard to pick up.

Shortly after my return after the holidays, I placed an ad in the local paper for a home for Bingo. Right away a family called who wanted the dog. But they agreed to take him only if I would accept their unwanted cat. And so that is how I ended up with having four cats. Buddy joined my family and helped absorb some of the hurt I still feel about having to give Mr. Bingo away.

_S/..J℄_

11

Events

Throughout my life I have experienced numerous episodes of the paranormal kind, which I call "events." The following are some of those events that took place while I still lived in the East.

The deer in the park

Once with a friend I went to a large city park. We drove up and were about to get out when this big beautiful deer came right up to my side of the car and he kept staring at me. I told Barb, "Stay here. I'll be back in a few minutes. That deer wants me to go with him."

He had the largest eyes of any deer I had ever seen. I got out of the car and followed him, and as I did, the path in the trail in the woods got more and more foggy until we reached a clearing. The deer would stop and look to make sure I was still following him.

When we got to a clearing in the woods, the deer vanished behind some evergreens and there, in the center of the clearing, shrouded in a mist, was a large football on tripods with several people walking around it. The next thing I knew, I was getting back into Barb's car and she was waking up. She remarked about my nose, and asked why it was bleeding from the left nostril. I reached up and saw blood on my hand and then she said, "You said you would be gone a few minutes," and she looked at her watch and said, "It has been over a few hours." The sun had set.

After that, she never wanted to talk about going to the park or seeing that deer.

The mantis at the fair

Another event was with my companion, Stanley. We had gone to a county fair and it was getting dark. As we were walking I strayed away from Stanley and passed a fence leading to an old field. On the fence I saw a mantis that was large, about 5 inches long. I remember going into the field to another object that resembled a disk. There was a Mantis person standing beside the disk.

Mantises: Queen (L) and King (R)

The next thing I knew, I heard Stanley calling for me. When I got to him, he noticed I seemed dazed and out of it, and I can't remember why I left him, but I told him about the mantis insect and how large it was.

Indianapolis circle and helicopters

At another time I was with a friend who was going to Indianapolis. We were going through all these green farmlands and I noticed a shift in energy in a certain spot, so I asked her to slow down and I rolled the window down in the car and saw in a green field a large perfect circle in which the glass was flattened down. Then we drove on and the energy went back to normal.

We kept on going, then something caught our attention. Over near a warehouse-looking building was a black unmarked helicopter just sitting there. Its windows were all darkened and there were no numbers or anything on it. As we slowly drove by, I noticed there were four more of the same type of helicopters lined up alongside the first one.

Stopped clocks

Another friend and I were driving through Tennessee after I went there for a conference on UFOs, and two tiny balls circled the car's antenna and rapidly took off. She and I were very drowsy.

All of a sudden, everything seemed like it was in a warp or a time shift, for her car's clock had stopped and my watch stopped, too, as did hers. (I can't wear a watch for long as I make them speed up.)

The cloud cylinder

My friend Nancy and I were going downtown once, when she told me to look over the city at a large cloud. There by the cloud was a large cylinder, silvery with no wings. She kept asking over and over, "Why doesn't it have wings?" and "Why is it just sitting there?"

At that point, as we watched, it started on a straight path into another cloud and didn't come out on the other side. I remember Nancy grew real quiet and, instead of going downtown, she took me back to my apartment. It was several months till she phoned me.

The duck pond triangle

I was visiting a lady in our complex when I got the sudden urge to go outside and head toward the duck pond. When I went there, I noticed a pulsing coming from the air all around me. I looked up and noticed stars were blacked out in a triangle pattern, and as I looked, I saw a large black-bodied structure with a dim red light in its center and two red lights on each wing. It seemed to sit there and I felt I was being pulled up into it. I remember doing a drawing later, showing rows and rows of computer banks aboard this triangle.

The white window doves

There were two pure white doves with huge eyes. They would land on my window sill about once a week. Well, one time when they came, I happened to look into one of the dove's large eyes and I got extremely sleepy. I couldn't fight the wave of sleep.

When I came to, I saw it was dark and almost ten o'clock at night. It had been about dusk when the doves came to my window. I had a bad nosebleed from my left nostril.

The cylinder that discharged silver objects

I was walking down a sidewalk near my apartment building when something told me to look up. There, between two clouds, was a cylinder discharging several silver objects; then an opening like a camera lens of black opened in the blue area of sky. I remember seeing stars in that black lens opening, and the cylinder entered it, just like if you would slurp up a spaghetti noodle. It vanished and the lens closed, and then the silver dots scattered all over in different directions.

Later I learned that this was an interdimensional portal to connect this galaxy to theirs.

The two mantises

I was watching TV when I got an urge to take my trash out to the dumpster. It was summer and when you go outside there's a white wall near the front entrance of the apartment building. Well, I stopped as I got out of the building, and I saw two tiny fully formed mantises sitting near each other.

I need to mention here that I really love insects. I have never been afraid of things such as snakes and spiders, and I find insect life particularly interesting.

I took out my trash and hurried back to the mantises and gently picked them up and took them into my apartment. They seemed to want to get on my dolls, so I put each one on a doll.

That night I noticed a glittery shimmer in my room near my bed. Then the next thing I saw were two Zetis standing near my bed. They thanked me for something, and then the glitter vanished as did they.

The next day I searched all over for the insects but found no mantises. If Kitty Girl had found them, there would have been wings and other evidence left behind, but there wasn't any.

The probe

My friend Cathy was visiting me in my apartment. I was in the bedroom when she called me to come into the living room fast. She said there was a bird flying around in the living room. The windows had no cracks and the screens were not ripped.

I got her to calm down and gave her a tablet to draw on, then asked her to draw what she had seen. What she drew looked like a ball with helicopter blades on it. When I had walked into the living room, I had heard a whirring, buzzing sound and had seen a faint object disappear. It was fading out when I went in there, and it wasn't a bird.

I told Cathy, "It's a remote probe. I have seen them often in my apartment."

After that she wanted to know more about it and about my people, for I had told her what and who I am. She has believed ever since she saw that probe, which was over eight years ago.

Radio transmissions

When I lived in the East and was going to college, I lived

in a tiny apartment. This was long before the car accident and before I moved to that senior apartment complex. I used to have this large kitty that would come around every night and sit on the ledge outside my window and stare in. His eyes seemed to glow a golden color.

Also I would hear the radio station awhile, though none were turned on inside my apartment. I wondered if a tooth filling would account as a receiver for radio transmissions.

While living there, I was close to that park where I got hit by that car. I got an urge to go to that park about almost sunset into an area that had an off-the-road trail. As I walked down it, I heard this hum that seemed to get louder and louder the closer I got to it. When I got closer, I saw a huge aerial transmitter like what a radio staton would look like, and right above it was a circular, glowing object with a pole coming out of its side and touching the aerial. It then took off rapidly and the hum stopped.

TV interruption and hovering disk

While at the senior apartments where I lived after the accident, the following events occurred.

I was watching TV and the picture started to mess up. It lost color, etc. When the TV was acting up, I got the urge to go to the window, and as I looked I saw two airplanes, a Cessna type, and in the middle of the two planes was a glowing white disk with shafts of light extending to each inner wingtip of the planes. I watched them as they left. This was a late afternoon event and then the TV went back to normal.

At another time, I was doing art work and listening to the radio. The radio started to act funny, playing the same songs and commercials over and over again. This went on for a long time, it seemed. I continued doing my art work, but then got the urge to go look out the window. There, over a large tree, was a silver disk hovering. It rapidly left and the radio went back to normal after that.

I used to listen to my police scanner a lot and sometimes I would hear a strange message over it. "Uncle Fred Onion" was police jargon for a UFO. The police would talk about strange lights that were being seen over the suburbs and the city where I lived. On one of those occasions I was listening and three lights appeared over the duck pond at nighttime. They came together and then departed in three different directions, leaving sparks behind them.

The hole in the screen

Another time I was in my bedroom back in my former apartment in the housing complex, and I was awakened from sleep by a hum that seemed to come from my living room. I got up without turning on any lights and there in my living room was a straight, intense, red beam of narrow light like a laser, coming through my screen and into the room. And it hummed. When I looked at my screen, there was a tiny round circle in it, plus on the wall nearby there was another round hole.

I remember the maintenance man came over to fix something in my apartment a few days later and removed the screen and patched that hole. I hadn't called anyone to report the damage, and he didn't want to talk very much.

The lilac bush mantis

While living at the Rileys', I remember they had a lilac bush that was my favorite bush near their house. I used to love to sit under it while it was in bloom during springtime. One day, while sitting under it, I saw a green mantis come down from it. He jumped on my knee and then he went into the grass a few feet away from me. Then I saw this misty-like, glittery stuff begin to whirl around me and that lilac bush.

When I opened my eyes to look, the mist hurt my eyes. There stood a little man that resembled the man who had levitated me as a baby. He was about 5 feet tall and was gray with huge wrap-around eyes. We seemed to talk by telepathy and then he vanished and the hazy bright fog disappeared. There was no mantis to be found.

The cemetery event

This event also occurred years ago, when I lived with the Rileys. It was a summer day when I was riding my bike up a road near my house. There was this old woods across from the railroad tracks and I was curious about it, so I got off my bike and crossed the tracks and went into those woods. I noticed an area that seemed icy cold, yet it was warm around the rest of it. The woods were an old type of oak and evergreen.

As I walked, there seemed to be a trail and as I looked around I saw this white, misty fog around the woods. I started to walk up that trail and was soon in that misty fog. While in it, I noticed there wasn't any sound nor a breeze, although it had been breezy before I was in the mist. As I continued on, I suddenly saw what appeared to be a frontier town, with traders and pioneer people and their animals, yet no sound at all came from them. When I reached out to the people around me, they seemed to pull away in all directions, which was odd. Even the houses seemed to pull away. Understand that I don't use psychotropic drugs or hallucigens. That *wasn't* a hallucination as some are so eager to judge it to be.

As I walked up that trail more, the fog again became heavy and I suddenly got past the town, and it was sunny and I found myself again in the woods, where I could hear the birds singing and see that everything was back to normal.

When I turned around, that mist was gone as well as that pioneer town. I went into that old cemetery and noticed the stones were worn and of an old type, flat marble head-stones a few inches thick. Their numbers were almost worn off. When I left that woods, I felt out of it, as if I had had a strange episode with the time continuum.

The strangest thing is, we used to drive up that road. I was with Rileys then and those woods were always there. But when we went up that same road, those woods plus the cemetery seemed to vanish, being replaced with an open field. The railroad tracks were still there. I noticed something else, too. After that time shift anomaly, the trains didn't seem to run anymore on that track.

Dolly meets her fate

Mr. and Mrs. Riley had a Boston bull dog that I was very bonded to. Her name was Dolly. Dolly was my closest friend for about four years. It was my job to take her out to potty every morning. She had a fenced-in yard to go to. Dolly was a silly dog. She would graze grass like a cow.

Well, one day she took off and I couldn't get her into the yard. I searched all over for her and couldn't find her. The neighbors down the road said they had seen a skunk on the railroad tracks, which seemed odd — seeing a skunk in day-light wandering on the train tracks? Being that I am so curious, I couldn't resist the urge to go and look.

Later on I was in our big field and was calling her. I called her and then I saw a dog come running out of the woods that was on the property. When she got halfway across that field, she simply vanished into thin air! So I walked up the railroad tracks and discovered a hide and Dolly's remains on the tracks.

Sasquatch remains

It was winter and I was in the woods looking around a tree that had recently fallen over. I smelled an awful odor, like death all around. There was a heavy snow, but I could see large footprints that were too big to be a bear's, and we didn't have bears around anyway. Then I saw some reddish fur on the side of a nearby tree.

When I went back in for supper, I was yelled at for handling a dead animal, even though I hadn't even touched it. I didn't tell them about the large footprints that I'd found nor the red hair. I have believed it was from a Yeti, a large bipedal primate that is referred to as Bigfoot or Sasquatch.

Little Appalachia

At one time as an adult I lived in a small town which I won't name, but will refer to as Little Appalachia. The people there were old-fashioned and superstitious. I lived in a trailer. People had horses and ponies, and one day two of their ponies were found mutilated in a field several yards from their pasture. At that time there had been a lot of activity in that region concerning aerial objects and lights.

People in that area seemed to avoid me, for some reason. Several times lights were seen over my trailer and I wasn't seen for two days. Then, one day after a rain, I went outside and discovered in my yard two large pieces of pink meat with little hairs sticking out of it. This scared me as I didn't know if a neighbor might have planted a body in my yard to get me in trouble or what. I had never seen anything like it before. And I hate to think what it might have been.

Another incident that occurred in that area was when a neighbor came over and wanted me to go to a farmer's field with her. So I went with her and an irate farmer was there to meet us. He had a long gun on him and demanded to know who had ruined his crop. When I went and looked, I saw a beautiful circle design in his field. The energy wasn't normal energy. I told the farmer I had been at home and couldn't have made it.

Another time there was this lighted object that would hover over my backyard when I lived in that trailer. One day I discovered a big yellow circle, and several of the trees began to die. But the grass around the circle seemed to grow faster than the regular grass in the rest of my yard. The trailer started getting this strange white stuff that covered the bedroom walls like mold after the circle in the farmer's field and my yard appeared.

The Civil War house

I used to clean for a family when I lived in the big city back East. That was before the car accident in the park in 1990. Twice a month I would go and clean for them, and I earned about a hundred dollars a month doing it. Their house was an old mansion type with a large staircase that led upstairs. When I worked for them, I used to have frequent trouble with vacuum cleaners burning up and light bulbs blowing out every time I'd go there. Most things seemed to occur upstairs in the hallway that connected the four bedrooms and a bathroom.

It was a warm summer day and that city got very humid in the summer. This house had no air conditioning in it, but up in that hallway it was like being in a freezing room, although other areas of the house were hot and sticky like it was outside. It was on that day that I was cleaning there when I felt a rush of air around me from out of the blue.

I happened to look up from my dusting to see a small child running down the hallway into another room. The couple I worked for were retirement age and didn't have toddlers or young children. This child had on a white gown and blond hair — it was a little girl. I went to look for her but couldn't find her. But I noticed that in spots the hallway would be icy and then hot, icy and then hot again.

One day while cleaning the steps that led down that staircase, I saw someone in the kitchen. I thought it was odd that the man would be home from work so early, but I looked again and saw a tall man with a reddish blond beard and a blue uniform with gold buttons on his jacket. His beard was almost to his belt that he wore and in that belt hung a long slender sword. He wore black boots and a blue hat. As I watched him he turned around, then faded. He grew wispy until he vanished. I later saw who I felt was a widow-type woman in a long black dress, crying in the seldom used bedroom that had old pictures on the wall.

After these events I asked the lady, who used to work for a disease control center and was a scientist, about the history of her house. She told me it used to be a Civil War house and that someone who was a part of the Civil War had once lived in it. It was an old mansion done up like those Southern mansions, and I must have seen the apparitions that were still drawn there due to the old history of the house.

The buzzing probe

I was going to the grocery store early one morning and there wasn't any traffic in the parking lot. I heard this buzzing, like a big bee nearby. I looked up to see if I could find it. There, a few feet away from me, was this rod-like thing about the size of a small pencil, that stood there as if watching me. It was silver in color. Then it circled me a few times and took off very fast.

Nearby, where the store was, there was a tiny pond on a small hill. Sometime after this rod I saw a dark green circle that formed on the hill facing the pond. It was an almost perfect circle. I used to see orbs around that pond several times, and the ducks seemed to avoid the pond for some reason.

Run-in with M.I.B.s

While I lived in that neighborhood of Little Appalachia, I got the chance to go with a friend to Tennessee to a UFO conference. After I came back from it, I was going to the grocery store on my old two-wheel bike when I noticed there was only one car in the parking lot. It was a big black car and there were four people in it, men wearing dark suits and ties. One had a case on his lap and it had red, blue and green and yellow buttons on it that blinked on and off. He seemed to be interested in me as he held out this microphone-like device toward me. All these people reminded me of Secret Service agents, although there weren't any visits by the president planned in our area. Their suits looked stiff and they wore hats and glasses which seemed odd, especially on such a hot, muggy day.

I got nervous, so I went around the other side of the store, and when I came back that car was going up a side street that I knew the route to. So I followed that big black car up that road. I noticed it had no plates and its back window appeared darkened as I followed it. That car just seemed to vanish into nothing in plain view of me. I never saw another like it, and still don't know what it meant.

The green-blue chain in the field incident

While I was younger, I loved to catch grasshoppers in our field. One early morning, while that grass was still wet with dew and long, as it hadn't been mowed, I was outside with a jar catching grasshoppers. I reached down to catch a large green 'hopper and my hands touched a greenish-blue cord or rope that seemed to have a chain inside of it. I noticed that the rope was coming down from the sky and I couldn't find the end of it. I then noticed that the sun seemed to vanish as if it had gone behind a cloud. I looked up and saw a large disk sitting there blocking the sun, and the rope was coming from an opening on its lower rim. I felt myself growing weightless and going up with the cord.

The next thing I recall is that it was afternoon and I was being called to come to lunch. The rope and disk were gone. I remember Rileys were upset because I had a nosebleed.

Purple slime event

While living at the Rileys', I used to take out the table scraps and put them down in the compost heap we called "the hill." This was near the edge of the woods. One evening after supper I went to take these scraps out and there had been a heavy rain before. While going across the orchard of apple trees, I saw something that caught my attention. There on the wet ground was this shiny purple mass that seemed alive and slowly moving in the direction of a tree trunk. I got a stick and poked at it. It seemed to quiver and back away from the stick. It looked to be made up of a gelatin-like stuff with glowing threads in it.

The next morning I went out to see if I could find it and there was a blackened path leading up that tree and the bark was burned off. Later that tree died and a circle appeared around the tree trunk of dead grass. I remember the night before I saw a strange glowing cloud that was oval-shaped and not a thundercloud.

The strange satellite

This event went on for several years while I lived with the Rileys. Around sunset I used to watch the sky and on one evening I saw this circular pattern of gold lights that would turn sideways and rotate up and down and then turn back into a perfect circle. It seemed to make cartwheels in the sky and then get close and then go farther away. I thought later it might have been a satellite, but it was too big to be a satellite.

The gold lights brightened and dimmed in a sequence.

The lights or pillars in the night-time sky

One summer evening I was sitting in the front yard under a pine tree when I happened to see these bright pillars of light that seemed to come from darker-bodied objects in the sky. They would send down about two to three beams at a time and turn them on and off in sequence. I got the impression that the objects were searching for something in a field some distance away. This went on about three nights with the objects being stationary and sending down brilliant beams of light and swaying back and forth and turning them on and off. I didn't think any airplane would have anything that could do what these objects were doing.

The portal in my room

This event occurred while I lived in the apartment complex. One night while meditating and burning incense, I saw a grayish tube of energy appear near a wall and ceiling near my bed. I heard my father, Khinyeo, telling me not to look at it or go near that wall. Being curious, I disobeyed him and went over anyway.

The next thing I knew, I was going through a portal of some sort with bands of dark with stars in it, along with gray energy bands separating the dark layers with stars. The next thing I knew I heard evil laughter and an awful noise like people in misery. There in front of me were these evil gargoyle-like beings that looked like crosses of pigs and other creatures bred with humans.

Dad had to come and get me out of there. He said it was a portal leading to a lower dimensional level. After that I obeyed Dad and never tried to get too curious about those portals again.

The strange TV picture

One night I got tired of watching TV, so I turned it off. At first it didn't want to go off, which was weird, as it was a fairly new set, an RCA. When it did go off, I saw a strange image that seemed to linger for several minutes. I turned the lights off in order to see it better. The image was of two comets with long tails and about three disk-shaped UFOs above and under the comets.

A week after that event, I was out at night watching a large comet that was visible in the night sky. I got the message that the mother ship *New Jerusalem* was trailing that comet. The mother ship had come back to resume operations over this sector.

I later had a premoniton about a friend of mine who lived in another region of the city. I saw her leave and move to California to join a group and she wanted me to go with her, to help that group teach others about UFOs, and to prepare to board that mother ship with them.

In that premonition I saw a large empty house with no furniture except for a table with computers on it. In the vision I saw my friend Jackie there, but she seemed different. She had cut her long hair like a crew cut and she was dressed in a two-piece sweatsuit of dark black, along with the others in her group.

The next morning I turned on my TV to hear them talking about a group in California that was hoping to board a mother ship. I then knew the dream I had was a premonition.

More recent premonitions

My last premonition dream was about two brothers falling to the ground after being hit by airplanes. That was the night before 9-11 occurred. The "brothers" were the twin towers at the World Trade Center.

The last premonition I had was of me and my Dad aboard a ship during daylight. We saw a large comet slowly burning up and leaving a long trail behind it. I told Dad that that comet was odd, taking a long time to burn up. Dad then said, "The silver bird is injured. Her wing is hurt." And the event or dream ended.

The next morning I turned on the news to see what I thought was a comet in daylight. As I watched I learned that the silver bird was the space shuttle *Columbia* and her seven astronauts. Her wing was damaged after liftoff. Someone e-mailed me to send me a picture of a UFO seen in the sky near that shuttle. Dad told me later it wasn't a dream, and that we had accelerated our time frame and were really there observing that shuttle accident. I was drained for a whole week from that event.

Granny Gail's UFO sighting

Granny Gail, an Internet pen pal of mine, reported on the following event on a Web site in May 2004:

It was one evening in east Texas, around 5 p.m., when a man and his wife were traveling westbound on Highway 21 from Logansport, La., back to their home in east Texas. They were just about halfway between Center, Texas and Nacogdoches, Texas, when they saw a very brilliant white light in the western sky. It was not a star because it was way too early for stars or planets to appear.

Then they saw that the light was moving, and coming in their direction. It came from many miles away in the sky to where they were, in almost a flash, but actually probably about two seconds, and then it disappeared behind them.

The two looked at each other, puzzled, and the woman said, "What the hell was that?" to which the man said "F___ if I know." The woman turned to see if she could see it out the back window of the car, but didn't see anything, so they just continued on.

In only a few seconds the light came whooshing back past them, traveling back toward the west as fast as it had come before. Again the man and woman were amazed and looking at something they couldn't identify.

The light disappeared into the western sunset. But before either person could comment on the light, it appeared again and was coming toward them. This time it seemed lower and extremely bright. It went overhead, and the woman spun around in her seat to watch where it went but didn't see it in the sky. She leaned over toward her passenger window and lowered it down to look out. The light was above them and she was looking up at the bottom of it.

She excitedly told her husband it was following them. She again looked out the window and it was still there, following along above the car, several hundred feet in the air. As the woman watched, the light began to grow dim. As it got dim, she could make out a metallic object, round, and a brassy gold color. The light went completely out and there, hovering above them, was this gold-colored round object.

It followed along above them for approximately forty-five seconds, and then the light began to come back around it. The light grew and grew in intensity until it completely hid the metallic object. When the light reached its brightest, the light then sped off to the west again and was gone completely. They didn't see it anymore after that.

What's so fascinating about just another report like that? Well, when the man and woman reached home, the lady checked her e-mail on her computer. They had been gone all day, so there were several e-mails there. One was from a good friend, and the time stamp on it was a little after 10 a.m. that morning. It said :

"My father is going to show you something today, his ship. I love you, Granny. — SilverUFO"

SilverUFO is our own Golden UFO here, and I am Granny. I saw this with my own eyes as did my husband. We will never forget seeing what we did. Believe it or not. I don't have to prove any of this to anyone, because it was not shown to me and my husband for us to prove anything to the world. It was shown to us because of the friendship we have with the one who sent the e-mail. Fantastic and unbelievable story? Yeah, it is to anyone who didn't see what we say. Crazy old woman? If I am, then thank you, God, for letting me be crazy enough to see that instead of pink flying elephants.

SilverUFO, of course, was my Internet "handle."

The mystery of the missing hen

In June 2002, Ann wrote in *The Star Beacon* about an incident that occurred on the mesa while I was visiting.

It was growing dark on Saturday, May 4, and I was closing up my flock of Aracauna chickens for the night. The birds usually know when it is time to roost and I do a count and close them up, to keep them safe from predators. This particular evening I did a count, but came up one hen short. I counted again, then again, but one hen was missing.

Immediately I sent our dog, Ranger, out to find the missing chicken. (Starhawk) joined in the search, but we were unable to locate her. Afraid that another fowl had fallen to foul play, we decided to take a walk around the property on Sunday morning, to see if we could spot any "evidence," such as feathers or fox tracks. When predators strike, it is usually more than one time.

Sunday morning was bright and sunny, a perfect spring morning. Marcy (a.k.a. Sanni) was staying on the property in (Peggy) French's mobile home, dog-sitting while (Peggy) was out of town. We decided to ask Marcy to come on the walk with us. I told her that we were looking for the remains of the missing chicken.

"Did you look around the henhouse?" she asked. Well, of course I had. I explained that we had looked in all the obvious places. Most likely something had dragged her off into the woods and had a meal. Or an eagle might have swooped down and carried her off, leaving no evidence.

We walked through the woods and after a while Marcy said again, "I think you should look around the henhouse."

I again explained that it was unlikely the hen was around there, for we had already searched.

We had walked a while longer when Marcy said, "I really feel like the chicken is around that henhouse. Do you mind if I go look?"

I sighed and told her to go ahead and look, but (Starhawk), the dog and I would continue circling the boundaries of the property. Marcy went straight to the hen-house. It wasn't ten minutes later when we heard her crying at the top of her lungs, "I FOUND THE CHICKEN!"

I started running toward home. Marcy continued to cry out, "I FOUND THE CHICKEN!"

Finally, Ranger and I got there. Marcy pointed to a spot next to (Starhawk)'s tool shed, which wasn't far from the henhouse and barn. A hen was stuck between a cement block and the side of the shed, trapped and unable to move. By the looks of her, she had probably fallen and gotten wedged there the day before. Marcy had found the chicken.

"I kept getting that I was to look by a white stone," explained Marcy. "I kept saying, 'What white stone?' The voice kept telling me to look for it, and then I saw the cement block, and there was the chicken!"

(Starhawk) reached down and dislodged the bird from its torture chamber. She was exhausted from trying to escape and quite battered looking. We placed her in back of the horse trailer and gave her water and some food. She remained in there for a couple of hours, and then I set her free. She has been walking cross-legged ever since, and her feathers are still frumpy and stick out. But she is doing just fine. She earned her name that day: Lucky.

Thanks to Marcy's intuitive skills, the chicken was saved before it died there. Who knows how long it would have been before we found her remains? It pays to listen to our inner voice and to check out what our intuition tells us. We acknowledge Marcy's gift and thank her spirit guides for bringing back one of our flock.

My home world, Jadui

_S/. Jɾ_ɔ

12

The Home World

My home world is called *Tieu* or *Jadui* by Zetis. It's the closest to our binary stars that astronomers know as Zeta Reticuli 2. Our suns are separated 350 billion miles apart from one another. Both are Class G2 and G1 suns (for reference, Earth's sun is a Class G0).

Our home is about six times larger than Jupiter, which we call *Juippes*. There is no weather like you have here, other than winds, and water is found high up and is collected using advanced collection devices.

Tieu is a semi-arid world that's mostly desert. There are many mountain ranges scattered across the planet. The soil is reddish tan in color. Most people live under domed cities, where everything is recycled. The air is purified and water that is collected is also purified. Plants inside cities are grown by hydroponics.

There are large train systems that run a few inches above the tracks that are electrogravity controlled in conjunction with a central crystal rotor. Their rails are located a foot underground. There are two types of trains, a six-car unit and a twelve-car unit, pulled by something analogous to a locomotive on Earth. Also underground are vast hangar storage places for ships, and there are several underground cities as well. Mining is conducted on nearby moons for minerals used in ship building.

Most ships are assembled from molds in floating space

ports. Some ships are formed via a matrix technique. A ship is grown in a matrix similar to growing certain bacteria. Mother ships are built in space at large space ports. There is ground transport similar to cars, but they don't run on fossil fuels, they are controlled by electromagnetic units.

On *Jadui* the people live in colonies or several small villages lumped under domed structures called *vadins*, which are large, glass-like biodomes where everything is recycled. Outside the atmosphere is too hostile unless you are in suits or ships. Zetis don't rent their homes, for their society provides for them. Each unit or family is allotted a place to put up their home, which is round or a bubble, and is located above ground on tripods. Their ships are stored in underground hangars.

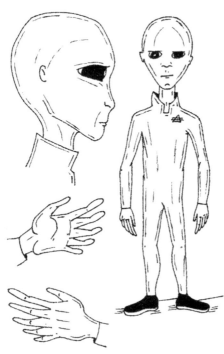

Zeta Reticulan anatomy

The people on *Jadui* don't live like Earth people, for their society is far ahead of Earthlings at the present time. Marriage is called *Tien-sieue* and is initiated when children are about 4 in Earth years, with an initial prearranged meeting called a *Galimi,* where they are bonded by energy exchange and aura bonding. Then, several years later, they are reunited for the actual *Tien-sieue* ceremony itself. *Tien-sieue* lasts about two of your Earth days.

People on *Jadui* don't reproduce as the Earth people do, for their genitalia are smaller and internal like other insectoids and, due to the wars caused by Blonds and Reptoids eons ago, made the people infertile, so they rely upon cloning and petri dish technology, and hybrid programs. A couple is allowed two units per family. People are assigned to various schools or academies for training in piloting a ship and things related to astronaut training. Zeti society has no sex discrimination and people are allowed to work and live without oppression.

Certain castes on Zeti Reticuli (*Jaduri* or *Jadui*) live in certain villages. The first is for scientists and engineers who are allowed one unit per couple, and that unit is trained to be a scientist as are its parents.

Their houses are large, communal, domed buildings and they are self cleaning as are the ships. Foods are replicated on board ships and inside the houses by food replicators that take the raw foods and process them. People who are designers and engineers live in communal dwellings and their ships are kept in underground facilities.

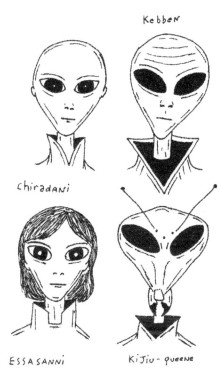

The different races of our world. **Essasannis** are the cross of Earth people with Zetis

Maintenance is done by two different means — biobots or androids. Biobots are special clones, and androids are robots designed to keep up houses, build and maintain cities, as well as work on crews aboard the large mother ships, performing maintenance.

There is a caste for pilots and astronauts — UFOnauts. They are rotated by Council to be on home worlds a certain amount of time per flight rotation and training — about six months on and six months off ship. Most of them live aboard their ships or on large mother ships, but when they are on shore leave from the ship, they live in domed, communal cities like engineers do.

Other castes include workers and farmers who live in

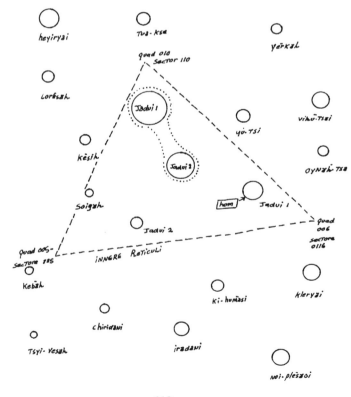

large colonies and grow foods and build cities. They live communally as well.

The map on the opposing page is a depiction of my home solar system: Our two suns, which human astronomers call Zeti 1 and Zeti 2, are binary suns. Zeti 1 is larger than Zeti 2, a dwarf sun, and both orbit each other. They are about 8 billion years old. Our closest planets are named after their suns.

My home is Zeti 1. We are 37 light years from your sun system. My people originated from advanced social insects — those related to mantises, ants, bees and wasps — but evolved longer than Earth and are an ancient civilizaton. There are about thirty different branches or species of my people.

Kebs are the tall Zeti, which is what my father is. Hybrids are called Essassani, which all Gray hybrids are. On the map, the lines are our trade routes to our neighboring star neighbors — *Tau Eridani* is a huge colony world where our hybrids that are created on Earth are currently stationed until Earth is remade into a paradise, and then they will be located here.

Gliese is a small world that orbits a red sun and is where Element 115 is created. *Gliese* is ten light years from my home. Element 115 is also produced on Alpha Mensa, which is 14 light years from *Jadui*, my home. Element 114, a byproduct of Element 115, is also produced there.

Element 115 is used as a propulsion fuel for several of our saucers. Some was given to Earth governments in a series of treaties among several nations. Element 115 was to be used for peaceful aviation purposes only and not in your military jets or in war. Half of Element 115 was removed from your nations and we ended our treaties in the mid-1990s with USA, Great Britain and Germany, because they violated provisions of the treaties about using technologies we exchanged with them for having underground bases for our saucers.

Our people are ruled by the hive, a large single mind, just as your ants and bees are ruled on Earth. We have a queen or a caste system as your social insects do; this is the hive. All Zetis are scientists and our society is built upon science and interstellar flight. We are time travelers, and when we visit Earth, it is our people's past as it was millions of years ago on my home.

Our caste includes workers and biobots, androids, teachers and the very tall Mantis people — the Elders of our kind. Then there are talls who make up our pilots and technicians on ships. Then there are Kebs that are commanders and admirals who fly ships. Essasanni is the hybrid class that serve as pilots and work on mother ships, in hangars and other areas of the ship, to be scientists.

A day on my home world is three of your Earth days. The atmosphere is slightly different than on Earth, composed of mostly argon and helium along with oxygen; it's not as heavy as Earth's. Our home is primarily cool desert, and we have two bodies of fresh water from where we grow our main foods under soil and water.

Reptilians are from Andromeda, Sirius and Antares. There are shape shifters on your Earth now passing as humans, and their mission is of control and
wars. Draconians are the group brought here from another solar system by the head Reptoid admiral a long time ago. Reptoids, along with Blonds, destroyed my home by nuclear war long before Earth was created.

About Ground Transport

Cars have a dome that slides up and you step into the car. There are two classes of cars, a V-car, which is similar in size to a van, and the smaller B-car, which has room for four people. Traffic is controlled by a magnetic interface structure that avoids your traffic jams. Roads on *Jadui* aren't visible as inside the cities there are lawns and park-like areas. Only outside the domed cities is the region arid like your deserts. Also cars operate by two ways — electro anti-gravity and by storing the energy from our suns inside a power cell-type battery.

About the different types of ships used by our people

First are the mega mother ships. These are floating cities that can remain away from port for several of your years, if possible. Large mother ships can't enter a planet's atmosphere as they are too massive. Propulsion is usually by nuclear reactors and a large "mega" might have twenty-four reactors aboard to power the entire vessel. A "mega" has a crew of several thousands of people plus android or drone staff.

Some "megas" are completely operated by machines only and have only a few hundred crews aboard them.

The next class is the explorer type mother ships which are medium-sized and can enter a planet's atmosphere if required to. Explorer types are powered by fission reactors and have about twelve cells aboard them to generate their power. Explorer types must occasionally take on supplies from the larger mother ships.

The next class are the servicers. A servicer is a small mother ship that is used as a supply vessel to stock the larger vessels. They are like a space barge and are completely crewed

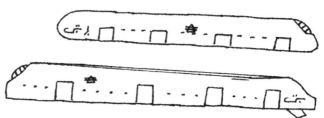

by drones and have no crews of our people to operate them. They are controlled by an on-board computer system linked to a central switching station or main computer.

Next are the space ports or docks. These are similar to what you have at your water transport docking facilities on your oceans. They are used for the large ships when their assignments are being rotated and crews exchanged and transferred.

The next class are the saucer class or *Vifami* (saucer)

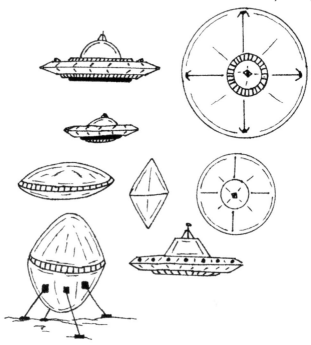

ships. These are the most common type of craft, coming in several sizes, depending upon their mission.

After the saucers are the delta wings or *Tibasi* or *Tibau*, which also come in different sizes according to missions.

Next are the *Ijonav*, which are a boomerang type of craft that comes in two sizes, large and small. These are used for reconnaissance and surveillance purposes. Some large *Ijonavs* are remote-controlled drones operated via computer connected to a mother ship's main computer system.

The next class are the *Ziavos* or *Ziamo*, which are a round ball to diamond-type ship. Usually they are operated by drones or via remote control from a large mother ship.

Next are plasma balls and plasma ships, which are intelligent orbs designed to record information about a planet's atmosphere. Some are programmed to be like cameras, to take in information. These were your early foo fighters in your WW1 era and WW2 era.

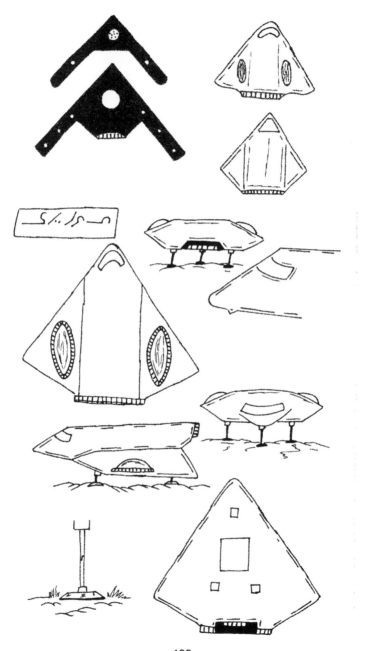

Afterword

When I returned to Roswell and the site of my crash in 2002, I received forgiveness from my Council, and they restored my rank once again to Commander. At that time I had the opportunity to return home, but I decided to stay as my educating people about UFOs and their reason for being here is important to the people of Earth.

I feel I must help them prepare for when the UFO coverup will be lifted and all nations, all governments will have to admit to the reality of UFOs and their crews, and the fact that others like me are living among humans and resembling one of them in order to observe their culture and their planet, while in reality we are E.T.s.

We are studying Earth and your society as a whole, and comparing it to other planets' societies and cultures as a yardstick to rank that planet's progress or lack thereof.

The interest of the UFOs and their crews is for your people to learn to end wars and oppression of all races, for the betterment of all humanity, and that some day people of Earth will be united with those of us from the cosmos.

Ultimately, we are connected as one with the family of man and of the essence of the stars and universal consciousness of the Creator, Yahweh.

On behalf of our people, we send our blessings of divine peace and universal love to the peoples of Planet Earth.

STRANDED ON EARTH

UFOs over the Ohio River

This photograph shows several ships that weren't visible when the picture was shot. Notice the cylinder-shaped object above center — possibly a mother ship. The picture below has been blown up to show this object in more detail.

STRANDED ON EARTH

The Author

Many people will "react" to what has been disclosed in this book. I suppose that is human nature. We question those things that our minds cannot fully comprehend, that seem to be outside "the norm."

I have known Sanni Ceto personally for five years now, and she lives a simple life in a small community, filled with challenges because of physical limitations and a past of misunderstanding and abuse. Despite all that, she has made many friends. She loves animals, plants and rocks, and that fact is undebated when you visit her home. She is filled with a loving nature and cannot understand why people are so cruel as to pin labels on others or accuse them of being untruthful.

Her extremely sensitive nature has made her both vulnerable and in need of constant reassurance. After all, it isn't easy coming to a planet filled with inhabitants that are often hostile and quick to judge. I give her credit for bearing all these years among humans, and I am honored to know her and to call her my friend. She is a highly intelligent being, willing to share her knowledge which she retained from her previous lifetime as that unfortunate Zeti pilot.

Sanni does not use alcohol, nor does she take drugs of any kind, and she has not written this book in order to draw a lot of attention to herself. As a matter of fact, putting this book together has dredged up a lot of pain and memories for her, and I commend her for having the courage to tell her story, and risk the ridicule of those who are unable to expand their minds to even conceive of the possibility that E.T.s truly are among us on Earth today. I am convinced that Sanni is one.

— *Ann Ulrich Miller, Publisher*

127

Printed in Great
Britain
by Amazon